THE MARGINS OF EUROPEAN LAW

Also by Ian Ward

A CRITICAL INTRODUCTION TO EUROPEAN LAW

LAW AND LITERATURE: Possibilities and Perspectives

The Margins of European Law

Ian Ward
Professor of Law
University of Dundee

First published in Great Britain 1996 by
MACMILLAN PRESS LTD
Houndmills, Basingstoke, Hampshire RG21 6XS
and London
Companies and representatives
throughout the world

A catalogue record for this book is available
from the British Library.

ISBN 0–333–67011–6 hardcover
ISBN 0–333–67012–4 paperback

First published in the United States of America 1996 by
ST. MARTIN'S PRESS, INC.,
Scholarly and Reference Division,
175 Fifth Avenue,
New York, N.Y. 10010

ISBN 0–312–16150–6

Library of Congress Cataloging-in-Publication Data
Ward, Ian, 1963–
The margins of European law / Ian Ward.
p. cm.
Includes bibliographical references and index.
ISBN 0–312–16150–6
1. Law—European Economic Community countries. 2. Europe–
–Economic integration. I. Title.
KJE947.W37 1996
341.24'22—dc20 96–15989
CIP

---

10 9 8 7 6 5 4 3 2 1
05 04 03 02 01 00 99 98 97 96

Printed and bound in Great Britain by
Antony Rowe Ltd, Chippenham, Wiltshire

For Clare

Contents

Preface

This is a book about the 'other' bits of European law. These are the bits which are all too easily ignored in contemporary studies of European law, all too easily marginalised. At the same time, and this is certainly no coincidence, this is the law which tends to relate most immediately to the individual in today's Europe. As its title hopes to convey, this is not a book about mainstream European law. The pretended formalism of mainstream European law, such as competition, free movement and agriculture, has already been successfully debunked (Snyder, 1990). This book does not devote itself to mainstream European law matters, and neither is it prepared to take a mainstream, and essentially uncritical, approach. It is a book which seeks to provoke, because it seeks to emphasise the injustice and inconsistency of the legal and political ideology of the new European order. Like all critical studies, it seeks, not only to emphasise these injustices and inconsistencies, but also to provide a reconstructive alternative. There is a virtue in being critical for the sake of it, but there is also a responsibility, wherever possible, to encourage something better. Regardless of whether the reader will sympathise with the tenor of the arguments that follow, I would hope that it can be universally agreed that the Community and its legal system could be doing so much better. Complacency and sycophancy are the two greatest dangers in today's Europe, not scepticism or critique.

The chapters which constitute this book are free-standing and discrete. There is no overall 'story'. Indeed, the lack of an overall story itself emerges as a particular characteristic of the new Europe. There are, however, certain common themes, and each of the four parts of the book is concentrated around the development of a particular theme. Margins denote definition and identity, and one of the themes of this book is the failure of definition and identity in the so-called new Europe. Part I, containing the first two chapters of the book, will concentrate on this lack of identity. The first, introductory, chapter will present the case for a sceptical critique of Europe and European law. More particularly, it will suggest the necessity for a critique of the particular 'idea' of Europe which enjoys contemporary dominion. Euro-scepticism is too easily castigated as being somehow anti-European. I would suggest that a scepticism of Europe and European law is vital if the European project is to be developed any further into the next millenium. The dangers of fragmentation and dissolution in Europe are only too apparent. The failure of identity is a critical one. The second chapter develops these themes by emphasising the historicity of the Community and Community law. Identity is entirely contingent upon history, and it is, at least in part, the failure to embrace history which constitutes Europe's failure of identity.

In jurisprudential terms, the failure of identity is most readily apparent in the constitution of Europe. Part II, containing chapters 3–5, concentrates upon the theme of the limits of constitutionalism in Europe. Chapter 3 considers the constitution after Maastricht, and seeks to suggest that the widespread criticism and disappointment articulated by so many (legal) integrationists can be better understood in the context of the peculiar history of the relationship between the Community and the nation-state. The European constitution is ill-defined, perhaps even inadequate (at least with regard to its pretended ambitions) because of the failure to define properly this pivotal relationship. This theme is developed in the following chapter, which seeks to investigate the nature of European legal integration; a crucial component in a European Community which was always intended to be integrated 'through' law. The problems of legal integration have been no greater than in the UK, and chapter 4 seeks to use the UK experience as an example of the 'limits' of European legal integration. Just as there is a limit, or margin, between the Community and the nation-state, so too is there a limit, or margin, between the law of the Community and that of the nation-state, and it is no less ill-defined. Chapter 5 addresses a collateral constitutional issue, which is again a problem of identity and definition. The Union constitutional order seems incapable of resolving the immediate problems of democracy, legitimacy and citizenship. Their resolution, it is suggested, depends upon a willingness to embrace radically alternative ideas and definitions of what democracy and citizenship can mean in a new Europe.

The law matters most to those who exist at its margins. This book is also about those who exist at the margins of European law; the dispossessed, the excluded, the marginalised. It is not, as I have already suggested, a book that concentrates on the heart of European law. It is, however, a book that concentrates on those who are most immediately disadvantaged by it. The condition of the individual has never been paramount in the new Europe. Indeed, as we shall see, repeatedly, it is only with the widening ambitions of the later 1980s and 1990s that Europe has tried to present any sort of 'human face'. In Part III, there are three chapters which consider particular margins of law, and at the same time, inevitably, the fate of particular groups of individuals who exist in these legal margins. Thus, chapter 6 will examine the status of Europe's 'others', immigrants, asylum-seekers and third country nationals, chapter 7 will concentrate on the position of women in the new Europe, and chapter 8 will investigate the extent to which the Community and Union are justified in claiming to respect human rights.

Ultimately, the concluding theme of this book is that a concern with margins is a concern with a particular development in contemporary theory. In the final chapter this theme is further identified as a post-modern concern. The new Europe, I would suggest, can be perhaps best identified as a post-modern entity, politically, culturally, socially, and so on. Its very lack of identity is itself post-modern, but rather than being something to be regretted, I will suggest that such an entity is to be embraced. Post-modernism is ultimately about justice. A post-modern critique of Europe and its laws can reorient jurisprudential investigation away from law and legalism and back towards justice and fairness. This is the potential which the new Europe enjoys and for this, if nothing else, it is to be applauded. Indeed, it may well be that the new Europe can perhaps best develop a distinctive identity in precisely this way, by identifying itself with justice. But it will need to be a very different Europe if this is to be the case, and it will, above all, need to be a much more critically aware Europe.

Acknowledgements

I would like to take the opportunity to thank a number of colleagues who have read various parts of this book, and with whom I have enjoyed discussion of a number of its themes. My greatest gratitude is to Clare McGlynn for her many incisive observations. I am also grateful to Tamara Hervey for her observations on chapter 7, and to the participants of the 'Europe's Other' Workshop at the 1995 Critical Legal Conference, to whom I gave a preliminary version of chapter 8. I must also take the opportunity of thanking the following editors for their permission to republish material, the *Oxford Journal of Legal Studies* (chapter 3), the *Liverpool Law Review* (chapter 4), the *Journal of Law and Society* (chapter 5) and Tamara Hervey as editor of *Sex Equality in the European Union*, Chancery Press (chapter 7).

Part I

Scepticism, History and the Idea of Europe

1 Raising the Spectre of Scepticism

Scepticism is a dirty word in European studies, legal or any other. The so-called 'Euro-sceptic' is pigeon-holed, castigated and marginalised. As Joseph Weiler has recently observed, in European studies, the 'moral high ground' seems to be 'occupied fairly safely by the integrationists' (Weiler, 1991b, p. 427). Perhaps this is why there is so little critical commentary in European studies, and European legal studies in particular. In legal circles, the idea of Europe is a given. The absence of a sceptical, or even a critical, voice in European legal studies should be a cause for concern. Yet the absence hardly seems to register. Despite the obvious absence of any normative order, save for a raw economic one, ironically European law has emerged as the bastion, perhaps the only remaining bastion, of unchallenged and unrequited legal formalism. In this introductory chapter, and throughout this book, I want to invigorate the sceptical voice. In doing so I am consciously echoing a wider sceptical movement in legal studies, which has characterised the critical edge of legal theory during the past two decades. It is now a commonplace in critical legal studies to emphasise the contextual nature of law (cf. Hunt, 1993). Law is at once politics, sociology, language, history, and so on. This is no less the case in European law than in any other legal study. As such, as my argument progresses, the ideas of a number of critical legal thinkers, and their intellectual mentors, will be introduced. I shall refer repeatedly to the ideas of such as Jacques Derrida, Drucilla Cornell and Richard Rorty. This is not just a matter of choice. It is an inevitability. Scepticism, as Rorty emphasises, is not an option. It is a reality of the human condition writ larger in our present post-modern condition (Rorty, 1989). This sceptical, critical, voice will not be directed simply towards Europe. I am not sceptical of Europe. Europe is; though what it is is more uncertain. Rather, I am sceptical of the 'idea' of Europe. Again, this is not a scepticism of any idea of Europe, but it is a scepticism of the particular 'idea' of Europe which enjoys current ideological reverence. More particularly still, I am sceptical of the role which the law has played in bolstering this 'idea' and defining it.

1 THE IDEA OF EUROPE

Clearly there are different kinds of scepticism, some more credible than others, and I shall introduce some of these kinds later in this chapter. First, however, I think that we need a clearer sense of what actually is the currently dominant 'idea' of Europe. It is primarily and distinctively a political idea, with a political ideology which has been stridently reaffirmed by the so-called '1992 Project'. As Weiler suggests, it is 'a highly politicized choice of ethos, or ideology, of political culture' (Weiler, 1991b, p. 430). What distinguishes the idea, then, is a political ambition. The Treaty framework is testimony to this. It is triumphed as the constitution of the European Community and Union. The very title of the political 'idea' is instructive. Not because it claims to be a Community, or a Union, although as we shall see subsequently, this uncertainty is itself instructive, but because it claims to be 'Europe'. Those not in the Community or Union are non-Europe, such as Norway, Switzerland, Poland and so on. These countries are no longer defined as European, at least not politically. The political identity is only one identity amongst many, and I shall return to the alternatives shortly, but it is the dominant and distinguishing identity of the Community and Union.

The Treaty framework does not, however, tell the whole story, or indeed, notoriously, much of the story at all. The current 'idea' of Europe is something more. As an idea it must pre-date its political and constitutional resolution. The idea is an idea projected and articulated by individuals. A paradigmatic text here, I would venture, is Ernest Wistrich's *The United States of Europe* (Wistrich, 1994). It is not that it particularly reflects the ambitions of Europe's politicians, although it probably does for at least some. Rather, it articulates a particular mission statement for the more committed 'pro-Europeans', who, as Paul Howe has recently suggested, can be identified as those who, in the present state of uncertainty, advocate the recognition of a European 'state' in order to generate a dominant sense of Europeanness (Howe, 1995, pp. 33–4). As I shall argue repeatedly through this book, and particularly in the final chapter, what we are really talking about here is a struggle over identity. The idea of Europe as a 'United States of Europe' is not, of course, new. Indeed, its strength stems as much from its historical authority as it does from any immanent viability. Monnet talked of a 'United States of Europe', and before him it was projected by the British Union of Federalists, an organisation which provided much of the intellectual fuel for the likes, not only of Monnet, but of Spaak, Spinelli and Schuman (Ransome, 1991). As the next chapter will reveal, the origins of the idea of a federal Europe are very much British. Indeed, Wistrich himself pays homage to this genus for the idea of a United States of Europe (Wistrich, 1994, pp. 18–21). Writing in the wake of the Maastricht Treaty, Wistrich suggests that there are now 'all the essential ingredients for an eventual federation' (ibid., p. 14). Such a federation, he contends, is the only alternative which can respond to the present legitimacy crisis which pervades our post-nation-state world. Whether we are really in a post-nation-state world is contentious. As I shall suggest in chapter 3, some would counter that the rumours of the death of the nation-state are somewhat premature (cf. Milward, 1992). For Wistrich the effecting of this 'eventual federation' will represent the realisation of the European 'idea'. The ideal constitutional models, he suggests, are those of Germany and Switzerland; the latter being an ironic selection, as it is no longer part of the newly redefined Europe. These two models are ideals of federal democracy (Wistrich, 1994, pp. 98–9). The emphasis on democracy is important. The present crisis in public disillusionment towards the European idea can be attributed, according to Wistrich, to the democratic deficit. Therefore, the 'first and foremost objective must be to correct the democratic deficit' (ibid., p. 165). Federalism is 'demanded' by the peoples of Europe as a response to the wider social impulses that pervade the continent. Echoing much of the familiar rhetoric of leading pro-Europeans, such as Jacques Delors, along with the inevitable intensification of the Common Market, Wistrich suggests that there must also be a common European 'social space' (ibid., p. 101). There must be both social cohesion and political citizenship.

The idea of political citizenship has emerged, since Maastricht, as a kind of totem. Much stock is set by the potential of citizenship to awaken the apparently dormant idealism of the peoples of Europe. Everyone appears to have their own idea with regard to what this citizenship should be. The Maastricht idea of citizenship, as I shall suggest in chapter 5, is a strikingly political and thus inevitably exclusionary one. Exclusion and marginalisation are in the nature of political determinations. Julia Kristeva has emphasised the degree to which political citizenship is an essentially modernist mechanism for politicising nationalism (Kristeva, 1993, p. 25). Soledad Garcia has similarly stressed the extent to which, in the modern age, citizenship is used in order to refine 'frontiers' and establish legitimacy (Garcia, 1993, pp. 21-7). A number of commentators, as we shall see, have countered with a form of 'new' or 'social' citizenship. Wistrich, for the record, suggests that citizenship should be constitutionally based on a human rights foundation; a fairly common line. This is then embellished by a second rather contradictory, if not frightening, qualification, whereby citizenship might be determined by tax-paying capacity, so that the only real European will be an employed European (Wistrich, 1994, pp. 81, 94). It is difficult to imagine any determination which could more effectively marginalise and exclude. Goran Therborn has made a similar and related observation, emphasising the extent to which the current European 'idea', like all the ideas of the past centuries, is a consciously 'elite one', seeking and drawing the support of the wealthier classes and the wealthier regions (Therborn, 1995, pp. 229–49). If the new Europe enjoys any identity, it is a blatantly middle-class one.

A supplementary suggestion, and one articulated by Wistrich, is that the new European citizen will better identify with the new Europe by means of cultural citizenship; he or she must be made to feel more culturally European. There must be a 'cultural space' to complement the political and social spaces. This will be determined by such things as the free movement of fine art and youth orchestras (Wistrich, 1994, pp. 90–1). The thesis is, of course, as absurd as it is objectionable. Whilst it might make connoisseurs of Reubens and Mozart feel a little more at home, it will do precious little for anyone else. European citizenship will not only be restricted to those who pay tax, but also to those who choose to spend what is left of their earnings on art galleries and orchestras. The attempt to create a European cultural consciousness by such means could be easily dismissed as indeed absurd, if it were not for the fact that this is precisely what the Commission has consistently supported as a means to creating a European identity. The Adonnino Committee suggested similarly that the idea of Europe could be semiotically complemented by such things as a European flag, a European hymn and, if funds permitted, a European space station. Wistrich concludes his thesis by suggesting that it is for 'opinion-formers', including not only TV and radio media, but also academic commentators, to refine the idea of Europe and to convince people of its innate veracity (Wistrich, 1994, p. 168). The struggle against the dark forces of scepticism is indeed a propaganda war.

It is not, however, culture which defines the current idea of Europe. Culture is not particular to it; though, as I shall suggest shortly, it may be partially co-determinative. What really effects this particular dominant 'idea' of Europe is law. Europe is not new, though we hear much about the 'new Europe', and neither are the various claims to a European cultural tradition. But European law certainly is new. Whether or not the European Community or Union, as established in either the Rome, Single European or Maastricht Treaties, actually is federal or confederal matters less than the fact that it is certainly something more than an intergovernmental organisation. The presence of the law, and its associated doctrines such as supremacy and direct effect, which together realise a rule of law, distinguishes this particular European 'idea'. Here are all the trappings of an essentially modernist legal order, and with it have come all the complementary trappings of a modernist jurisprudence. Legal commentators talk about rights in Europe, they worry about sovereignty and supremacy, and the balance of power. Everyone searches for normative orders. The most recent substantive and influential attempt, by Joxerramon Bengoetxea, is a classic example of such an approach (Bengoetxea, 1993). Implicit in such a thesis is the ready assumption that a jurisprudence for the new Europe can be analysed in the light of certain preconceptions derived from orthodox modernist jurisprudential traditions.

Rather than take the opportunity to explore radically alternative theoretical approaches, all too often there is a recourse to comparativism. Just as the political scientists try to identify federal or confederal qualities in the political 'idea', so too do legal commentators try to identify federal or confederal qualities in the legal 'idea'. The paradigmatic texts here are those presented in the influential *Integration Through Law* series, the thesis of which explored the popular idea that the law has paid a key role in the integration of the Community. Indeed, lawyers frequently express a pride at the way the law has been able to keep the flame of integration burning bright, even when politicians have seemed unable or willing to do so. The establishment of the European Court of Justice at the apex of the Community's institutional structure is often taken as some sort of implicit signal that the founding fathers of Europe always intended for the Community to be integrated by lawyers. Then with supreme unconscious irony, in the very next breath, the same commentators often bemoan the apparent lack of democracy in the new Europe (cf. Mancini, 1991).

The authors of the *Integration Through Law* series characterised their project as 'functional' as opposed to 'theoretical'. The greater the role of the law, they concluded, the less need for philosophical diversions (Cappelletti et al., 1985). Comparative law can be used as a means of avoiding having to think originally about Europe. The suggestion that there might be a radically alternative, post-modern, political and constitutional theory is never taken seriously. Some sort of modernist, federal variant is taken to be unavoidable. The consolidation of a modernist European constitution was clearly evidenced at Maastricht. Significantly, the welter of criticism which was levelled at the Treaty by legal commentators almost exclusively centred on perceived failings to conform with modernist expectations. Thus there is much anxiety about the apparent failings of representative democracy, the so-called democratic deficit; the virtue of representative democracy is presumed. There is also much anxiety about the lack of congruence between political citizenship and legal rights; and likewise the immanent virtue of congruent rights is presumed. The Protocols are a cause of much concern, because they may not be justiciable and that would never do. And what of subsidiarity? To the clinical legal mind it lacks definition; but then it was precisely employed in order to circumvent the need for clear definition (cf. Teasdale, 1993, pp. 189–92). The new post-Maastricht Europe, it is concluded, does not conform to the classical tenets of a modernist constitutional order (cf. Curtin, 1993). Therefore, it cannot be right.

European law reinforces and indeed helps to define the particular 'idea' of Europe which enjoys contemporary dominion. It defines and identifies the new Europe. I stress this because I want to emphasise the power that the law wields in this ideological ambition. It is almost universally accepted that this is a good thing. The role of law in furthering the idea of Europe and European political and economic integration is applauded. It is good for law and good for Europe. But is it? It is good for Europe, only if the Europe that is projected upon us is the Europe that we really want. As I suggested at the beginning of this chapter, I am sceptical about this Europe, primarily, though not exclusively, because this idea of Europe triumphs all the exclusionary potential which typifies the modernist and essentially statist legal and political ideologies upon which it models itself. This is, of course, the central theme of all the chapters which make up this book. But before moving on to discuss these issues, I want to explore a little further the nature of scepticism in European studies.

2 A LITTLE EURO-SCEPTICISM

Euro-scepticism comes in many forms. There is no typical scepticism, but there are common threads. First, there is a shared concern about the prevalent 'idea' of Europe. It is the idea, as I have already stressed, that matters. No one is sceptical of Europe; such a scepticism would be absurd. Secondly, there is a common recourse to history. History breeds scepticism. Normative pretensions can always be undercut by historical awareness. What a historical appreciation of Europe reveals is the contingency of the present dominant idea of Europe. It is just one idea in a sequence of many, many ideas of Europe, some more loopy than others, some more tyrannical and dangerous than others, and some more feasible than others.

I shall discuss the more contemporary history of the dominant 'idea' of Europe, and its realisation, in the next chapter, but for now it is more revealing to concentrate on the longer historical view. A number of studies have recently engaged the historical perspective. One of the most challenging and persuasive of such studies is Gerard Delanty (1995). According to Delanty, Europe has always been 'an idea as much as a reality'. Europe has always invented and reinvented images of itself, and as such only exists as a kind of ephemeral cultural construct. There has never been any one immutable European identity. This, he terms, the 'ambivalence of Europe'. This very historical idea of Europe, he then continues, is very much more one of difference and change rather than unity and continuity. This tradition, he suggests, plays against the 'unifying myths of integration' which have gained contemporary currency. These myths have their origins in nineteenth-century Gramscian hegemony and its pretended universalism. Such a fiction nourished the idea of a 'fantasy homeland that goes hand in hand with a retrospective invention of history'. The immediate and obvious consequences have been the paradoxical association of the 'idea' with nationalism and the 'idea of nationality'. Europe has been imagined as a supra-state, codeterminative with the nation-states (Delanty, 1995, pp. 1–15). The thesis that the Community and the nation-states, rather than threatening one another, have actually ensured one another's survival will be developed in chapter 3.

The first of the 'ideas' of Europe, and the one which casts the longest shadow, is the Catholic idea of a Holy Roman Empire. Derek Heater has presented precisely the same thesis. Charlemagne was the first to style himself the 'father of Europe'. The papacy was the first actually to use the concept of Europe as an identity, cultural or political. The 'others', defined by this Catholic idea, were first, the external barbarians of Islam, and then, increasingly, the internal 'others', the Jews (Heater, 1992). Julia Kristeva identified Christianity as providing intellectual 'laboratories' for the metabolising of 'identification hatred' by the exclusion of those designated to be 'other' (Kristeva, 1993, p. 4). A complementary geographical margin emerged; the 'other', the non-European, lay to the east, beyond the boundaries of Catholic dominion. This identity shifted slightly during the modern period, and indeed modernity became synonymous with 'Europe'. Europe became a Europe distinguished by a geopolitics of nation-states operating in an economic regime resembling a common market (Llobera, 1993). Culturally, this Europe identified itself with 'progress, civilisation and Christian redemption'. It was this Europe which sent out missionaries. The Frenchman Dubois recommended the despatch of young and nubile European women to seduce and convert the heathen (Heater, 1992, p. 11). In the words of Margaret Thatcher, it was this missionary zeal which 'colonised and – yes without apology – civilised much of the world' (Paul, 1992, p. 53). The 'other' remained very firmly that identified by all things eastern, oriental and barbaric. There was therefore a certain cultural, economic and even political identity, defined as much by the 'other' as by any immanent rationality. But it was also a Europe of difference, dominated by the interests of nation-state and national interests as advocated influentially by the likes of Hobbes, Bodin and Bentham (Heater, 1992, pp. 39, 92–3). Precisely, of course, the Europe of today (Delanty, 1995, pp. 65–114).

The threat to this particular 'idea' of Europe comes with the twentieth century and the various technological and economic urges which have caused such intellectual anxieties about the perceived 'cult of progress'. Oswald Spengler's *The Decline of the West* was just the most notorious of a number of studies prophesying a post-modern Europe spiralling to its destruction. Influential philosophers such as Nietzsche, Heidegger and Jaspers wrote similarly, warning Europe that it was about to be devoured by the technological monster which it had created and by which it had defined itself (cf. Heidegger, 1977). The alienation of the individual lost in this technological modernity was a theme taken up by writers as disparate as Camus, Kafka and Orwell. Richard Rorty suggests that Orwell was the prophet of the twentieth-century demise (Rorty, 1989, ch. 8). Ortega y Gasset suggested that: 'The world today is suffering a grave demoralisation which, amongst other symptoms, manifests itself by an extraordinary rebellion of the masses, and has its origin in the demoralisation of Europe' (Gasset, 1972, p. 195). The idea of the alienation of the disoriented individual cannot be merely dismissed as history. Anthony Smith has recently described the situation in Europe today as one in which 'modern technologies and communications have led many people to question the old certainties'. As a result, we 'grope in some confusion towards a new type of social order, yet are afraid to let go of the old' (Smith, 1992, p. 56).

The pretended saviour of the European idea was fascism. It alone suggested that the essence of Europe might be salvaged by an economic union devoted to preserving the political and cultural prosperity of the historically defined 'European'. The 'idea' of Europe, throughout its various manifestations, can never be separated, according to Delanty, from 'European fascism', and its use of economic and geographical exploitation (Delanty, 1995, pp. 112–14). For Nietzsche it was a matter of realising Europe's 'destiny':

> What matters is the One Europe, and I see it being prepared slowly and hesitantly. All the vast and profound minds of this century were engaged in the work of preparing, working out and anticipating a new synthesis: the European of the future . . . the small states of Europe – I mean all our present empires and states – will become economically untenable, within a short time, by reason of the absolute tendency of industry and commerce to become bigger and bigger, crossing natural boundaries and becoming world wide. (Heater, 1992, p. 123)

Rather than representing any discernible change in ambition or image, the post-1945 Europe actually reflected a subtle intensification of the same evolving idea. It finally realised the dreams which had nourished the common ambitions of Charlemagne, Napoleon and most latterly Hitler; a European empire, founded as a capitalist super-state, self-supporting through a common economic market, founded on the exploitation of minority interests. As Heater concludes, the difference between Hitler's vision, or Marx's, and Monnet's is merely one of emphasis, rather than one of substance: 'Totalitarianism is bloated state sovereignty; federalism is attenuated state sovereignty' (Heater, 1992, p. 147). As a number of commentators have noted, post-1945 Europe is a Europe more than ever defined by the dominant ideology of the state, characterised by the various exercises in trying to create a complementary European state culture (cf. Delanty, 1995, pp. 126–8; Weiler, 1991b).

One of the further and defining characteristics of this new Europe is once again its identification of the 'other', the barbarian to the east, the would-be migrant who would take advantage of Europe's economic riches and presumed cultural superiority. Of the 340 million European citizens, 15 million are marginalised migrants, virtually all of whom are amongst the 50 million who can be designated 'poor'. Despite the veracity of their political, social or geographical claims to citizenship, as we shall see subsequently in chapter 6, their ethnic origins preclude them from ever being part of the 'idea of Europe'. Delanty refers to the 'new soft racism' which 'crystallises on the question of the inassimilability of non-European immigrants and speaks in the name, not of race as such, but of national identity and cultural boundaries' (Delanty, 1995, p. 154). The new European idea is, then, merely a variant of the traditional ideas which have evolved over centuries. It is still an essentially Catholic, conservative idea; one determined by ethnic, social and economic marginalisation.

The present variant on the 'idea' is ultimately a mythological projection, which attempts to present itself devoid of context, as a 'transcendent unquestioning symbol of Europe'. What is missing still is any alternative 'collective identity'. This is the crucial failure, the reason for which

> resides in the fact that the dominant concept of European identity pursued today is that of the state model. The mechanisms of integration that this promotes are based on enhancing bureaucratic control, political centralisation and economic crisis management. . . . Consequently, Europe is being 'imagined' or 'invented' as a memoryless

> bureaucratic macrocosm to protect life-worlds organised around patterns of consumption and welfare, and with nationalism still providing the necessary emotional substitution for deficits in legitimation. Today, then, the European idea has engendered a contradiction: the antinomy of political, economic and military integration on the one side, and on the other social and cultural fragmentation. (ibid., p. 132)

Europe has become a 'function of the nation-state', a discursive 'conceit', a 'myth'. It is the 'embodiment of prejudices which lie deep in the history of Europe'.

The solution which Delanty articulates is one common to a number of sceptical critiques of the European idea. In his opinion, there must be a 'post-national' European identity, determined by a 'politics of cultural pluralism', together with a complementary idea of 'post-national citizenship based on participation and solidarity'. The 'crucial issue here is the institutionalisation of pluralism' (ibid., pp. 157–63). The ideas of a post-national citizenship, participation and pluralism lie at the heart of many of the ideas which I shall project in the following chapters (ibid., pp. 9–12). In an eloquent passage, Delanty summarises a view shared by many sceptical of the present nationalistic and statist idea of Europe:

> it is difficult to deny that there is an element of mystification in the idea of Europe. It projects the language of the life-world and political struggles onto the macro-dimension of a community of states by the invention of a mega-community. The result is not genuine internationalism but a socio-technical framework for the exploitation of scarce resources and the pursuit of unrestrained economic growth. We find that the idea of Europe is becoming the driving force of strategies of macro-political and economic engineering, and, above all, the substitution of a new goal, closely linked to the neo-liberal political programme, for the traditional social democratic programme. It is a unifying theme which links the macro-level of economic and global frameworks to the cultural reproduction of the life-world and enhances the steering-capacity of the former. The most important task for Europe today is the articulation of a new idea of Europe

which would be capable of providing an orientation for a post-national European identity. Rather than being the leitmotif for 'disorganised capitalism' the European idea should, if it is to be anything, be the basis of a new politics of cultural pluralism. (ibid., pp. 8–9)

Delanty's critique is not presented because it is somehow the best or most appropriate. I would suggest that it is characteristic of a sceptical position, in just the same way that Wistrich's thesis is representative of those who advocate the 'idea' of Europe. Another, perhaps more renowned figure, who has presented a strikingly similar critique is Jacques Derrida. His essay *The Other Heading* once again isolates the dominant 'idea' of Europe, and deconstructs it both historically and textually. What Derrida is actually deconstructing is the discourse of Europe: its imagery and its semiotics. Europe, he alleges, has always been a symbol, a semiotic (Derrida, 1992, pp. x–xi, xlii–iii). The historicity of this semiotic is underlined by the very structure of the essay, built around a Europe of 'yesterday', of 'today' and of 'tomorrow'. The Europe of 'yesterday' was characterised by a critical potential in that it respected temporality and difference. The Europe of 'today' is seeking to ignore this potential; a futile but debilitating project. Europe singularly fails to acknowledge the temporality of 'today', and can thus neither distinguish itself from, nor determine itself through, its past (ibid., pp. 35–5, 12). The historical idea of Europe has always projected itself as a universal that is defined by its own 'differentness'. This is both an internal difference, between various cultural nuances and national interests, and an external difference, from the barbarian 'other'. By ignoring its history, the Europe of 'today' is seeking to erase this 'difference'. By failing to acknowledge the marginalisation of the 'other' in this way, it is committing the ultimate deceit. It seeks to 'forget' the 'other', just as it seeks to forget its past (ibid., pp. 24–5).

The raw politics of today's Europe is, then, a 'crisis of memory' (ibid., pp. 29–32). The crisis has two roots, which Derrida explores by his familiar mechanism of uncovering linguistic ambiguity. Indeed, the heart of his thesis revolves around the development of two particular words; *capitale* and *capital. Capitale* denotes cultural dominion, whilst *capital* denotes economic dominion. The cultural dominion of Europe has already been noted. It is a double-edged sword, as Derrida suggests, itself a 'contradiction', at once defining the spirit of Europe, but at the same time attempting to establish cultural homogeneity. This contradiction is ever-present, but must still be resisted. The ambition must be to 'invent' a medium between dominion and non-dominion. At present, in Derrida's perception, the pervasive European attitude is one of centralisation and the diminution of particularity through the appropriation of nationalism (ibid., pp. 47–8).The new European discourse is a discourse of capital and technology (ibid., pp. 50–5). The echoes here of Derrida's intellectual mentor, Heidegger, are clear. Capital, more than anything else, threatens Europe, because it threatens to establish an 'ethos' of capitalism. Capitalism is the weapon which threatens to champion universalism over differentness.

Moreover, it threatens to 'close off' the future, as of course does any teleological metaphysics. The future must be re-opened. The new Europe will be judged by its appreciation of difference, of the 'other'. Derrida suggests that we must search for an identity which includes respect for both universal values and for differentness. Only a truly pluralist discourse can defeat the centralising ambitions of political heterogeneity. Today's Europe has become ends-oriented. Pluralism will subvert any attempt to establish objective ends of the human condition. So we must, above all, come to appreciate again the 'experience' of 'antinomy'. 'Responsibility' demands of us that we continually seek definition and redefinition, and we can only do that by establishing 'exemplars' which are at once universal and particular. This is what Edmund Husserl defined as the European 'idea', the 'paradox of the paradox'; every universal is a creation of a particular individual (Derrida, 1992, pp. 72–5). 'Europe', at once, describes both a universal and a particular, and must define itself as such. It is, as Derrida urges, an 'interminable' critique, but also a necessary one. What we must do, above all, is avoid the disempowering which accompanies 'homogeneous discourse'. The idea of Europe, and its discourse, must remain critical and plural. What Derrida is advocating, ultimately, is a post-modern 'idea' of

Europe, and I shall return to this possibility in the final chapter.

A third and final sceptic whom I want to introduce at this point is Stanley Hoffmann, undoubtedly one of the most familiar and influential of sceptics amongst UK lawyers and academics. Although, as an American political historian and scientist, Hoffmann might, at first glance at any rate, seem to come from a very different background from that of Derrida, or even Delanty, what he says reveals a number of very striking similarities. Furthermore, a particular value in studying Hoffmann's writings is their time-scale, the earliest being written at the very inception of the Community, the later in the wake of the Maastricht Treaty. The consistency of the critique thus enjoys a particular resonance. Above all, what aligns Hoffmann's critique with those of Derrida and Delanty is its historicity and its concentration on the very idea of Europe and its crisis of identity.

Hoffmann emphasised 'identity' as the critical issue in his very earliest essays. In 'Europe's Identity Crisis', published in 1964, he referred to a Europe 'prosperous and disunited', caught between a series of tensions, attached to the old, attracted to the new, economically and socially fragmented (Hoffmann, 1995, pp. 9–50). Echoing so many commentators, he described a Europe which epitomised the alienated and dislocated world of modernity, which clung to its nation-state inheritance, but which yearned to break free by erasing its past. Ideologically, it was a 'silent' Europe, a Europe without spirit, lacking a belief in anything but the idol of capital, devoid of civic or political virtue. In intellectual terms, 'smart debunking' had 'replaced rash belief' (ibid., pp. 23–5). In the absence of an intellectual foundation or a political 'vocation', Europe had sought recourse in a vacuous '*projet*'; the realisation of a European state. This he termed the 'Monnet method', the bald assertion of supranationalism and neo-functionalism, and it was the 'most potent' of all the 'illusions'. Rather than being a theory, it was simply 'an act of faith'. Post-1957 Europe was no more united than before. If anything, the Community merely revealed to all the depth of Europe's disunity. In Hoffmann's words, 'the recourse to supranational integration by governments means only that they choose to conceal the embarrassment of dissension behind the businesslike façade of supranationality'. Supranationalism, he suggested, was, and is, the semiotic of national 'discord' (ibid., pp. 33–6).

Hoffmann returned to precisely the same themes in a review of this essay published in the aftermath of the Maastricht Treaty in 1994 (ibid., pp. 52–3). The essential arguments, he asserted, were still valid. Though perhaps more prosperous, Europe was even more disunited. The resolution of the Treaty had merely deepened a 'prevailing pessimism', brought about first, by the determination of the nation-states to preserve their status against any overt federal ambitions and secondly, by acute economic recession. Interestingly what the Europe of the 1990s reveals, Hoffmann adds, is a Europe which can be no longer and no further integrated by means of the European Court of Justice alone. The Court of the 'United States of Europe' has never enjoyed the hegemony afforded to its counterpart in the United States of America. Thus, whereas the 'Supreme Court succeeded because it was interpreting a Federal Constitution; the European Court of Justice's attempt to blow federalist air into weak lungs of a community based not on a constitution but on a series of treaties could not, by itself, suffice'. Europe in the 1990s must seek an identity beyond that which can be furnished by the received tenets of modernist jurisprudence (ibid., pp. 52–3).

Crisis, as it always has done in the Community, in the 1950s, the 1970s and again in the later 1980s and 1990s, had revealed a series of independent nation-states pursuing their own economic, social and political agendas. Strikingly, and worryingly, there has been a recourse to nationalism and xenophobia. Most worryingly of all, once again there is an intellectual and ideological vacuum. The 'idea' of Europe which enjoys current dominion is an anti-idea, an idea 'without ideology'. It is not arrant anti-European scepticism which threatens this hegemonic 'idea' of Europe; it is everybody's indifference towards its fate that really matters. The Maastricht Treaty served only to emphasise the depth of this scepticism, an awareness that much was wrong, but an unwillingness or inability to do much about it (ibid., pp. 54–62). The new European Union is thus a 'compromise between the inadequate and the impossible'; the inadequacy of loose intergovernmentalism and the impossibility of federalism. The realisation that federalism can no longer provide a model, rather than inspiring a new post-modern idea of politics, has led to a pervasive pessimism devoid of any ideology. It is a Europe at the 'end of ideology'. In a later 1979 essay, he used the metaphor of an escalator; the kind of machinery that when it seizes up no one ever seems to know what to do (ibid., p. 197). In its place there is a 'politics of fear' and a 'politics of meanness', revealed, as we shall see in chapter 6, most obviously in Europe's treatment of its marginalised 'others', but also present in each and every policy measure designed to complete the common market. The Europe of the 1990s, the Europe of rampant competition and exploitation, is in the end an 'unpleasant' Europe (ibid., pp. 65–6).

Hoffmann has developed these essential themes, challenging the myth of a Europe moving ever closer together, driven by a common ambition founded on a common ideology in numerous other essays. In the 1970s he concentrated particularly on the example of France as the nation-state *par excellence.* During the 1980s and 1990s, as we shall see in the next chapter, that mantle has been taken on by the UK. In an early 1960 essay on France's relation with the Community, he warned that a 'half-way' federalism was destined, ultimately, to be inadequate. Unless Europe moves completely beyond the nation-state, there will be no community, other than that which describes a sophisticated beneficial trading alliance (ibid., pp. 102–3). It has proved to be prophetic indeed. In 1976, he described the ambition of integration as a Sisyphean task, driven by the dynamic of capitalism, itself compromised by the disintegrational impulses of competition (ibid., pp. 107–35). Again, in 1989, he repeated the warning that a Europe of 'savage capitalism', to use Jacques Delors' own phrase, will serve only to increase the number, and disaffection, of the ever more marginalised economic losers. The '1992 Project', the semiotic of the new European 'idea', described the necessity of economic exploitation unhindered by social or political interests. It represented the abandonment of any identity other than the purely economic. If anything symbolises the 'end of ideology' in late twentieth-century Europe it is the '1992 Project' (ibid., pp. 229–45). In his most recent essays, Hoffmann has increasingly called for a new European idea and a new European political ideology, beyond the old confrontation of supranationalism and intergovernmentalism, and beyond the suffocating bureaucracy and institutionalism which has done so much to alienate the putatively new European citizens. Until such an idea emerges, there will be nothing distinctive about the so-called 'new' Europe with which anyone can identify (Hoffmann, 1995, chs. 12–13).

The reconstructive edge to each of these sceptical theses is that there must be a rewritten European 'idea', which can then redescribe a European identity. This has to be a post-modern writing, and I shall suggest such a writing in the final chapter. Goran Therborn situates the Europe of 1995 in the 'late afternoon glow of world modernity' (Therborn, 1995, p. 1). The new Europe can lead the world, not just itself, out of modernity and into post-modernity. Post-modernism challenges each of the characteristics of European modernity, Christianity, nationalism, nation-state citizenship, individualism and economically determined social class. The challenge of scepticism is to reintroduce difference, to advance the claims of multi-culturalism and multi-socialism, to deconstruct all the normative orders, social, economic and political, which underpin the modern idea of Europe (ibid., ch. 14). Echoing Hoffmann, Therborn places the new Europe at the 'end of ideology', or at least at the end of modernist ideology. The only ideology, the only identity, which it can now describe is a post-modern one. This, he suggests, will be an ideology of 'co-operation' which rests on a new, essentially discursive and textual, idea of Europe (ibid., pp. 360–6).

It might be thought that these concerns about the idea of Europe are somehow too distanced from the immediate realities of European law. The remaining chapters of this book will be devoted to debunking such complacency. The absence of legal commentary which seeks to develop these concerns in a jurisprudential context is indeed striking, as I have already tried to emphasise. However, the absence is not complete. Joseph Weiler has referred to the ironic threat of statist Europe, mythologically projected as a European 'Promised Land':

> It would be more than ironic if a polity and political process set up to counter the excesses of statism ended up by coming round full circle and transforming itself into a (super) state, and it would be equally ironic that an ethos which rejected the nationalism of the Member States gave birth to a new European nation and nationalism. (Weiler, 1991b, p. 435)

In a perceptive and revealing critique of the role of law in the affirmation of the particular idea of Europe, Philip Allott has emphasised the intellectual failing of lawyers assuming that European legal studies is merely an exercise in applied science, rather than appreciating that the law of the 'idea' is in fact a historical and interdisciplinary 'phenomenology'. The present crisis in Europe, he suggests, now demands a 'revolutionary change in the Community's consciousness of itself, a change which requires a new approach to the questions of its philosophical and historical significance' (Allott, 1991, pp. 2485–8). Echoing a number of the critiques already introduced, Allott further castigates the duplicity of Europe, using an idea of supranationality in order to mask a reality of nation-state hegemony and incipient statism. The Community, he emphasises, is the epitome of middle-class, white, prosperous Europe. His conclusions are apposite:

> The absence of a transcendent social framework for the Community power-system has generated a cascade of consequences in the constitutional development of the EC over the last forty years. It has meant that the EC system, a particular political and legal system, reminiscent of nation state systems, has come to be equated with the 'idea' of Europe for many people. It has meant that the EC has seemed to have no reason for existing other than the continued willing of the state systems of the states that found it. . . . This in turn means that there is a sense of retrograde motion in the development of democracy in Western Europe, as politicians and civil servants take over the negotiation of new laws as if they were negotiating treaties. . . . In British eyes, we seem to be reverting to the sixteenth century period of the Tudor constitution, when strong monarchs used the parliamentary system as

> a machine for policymaking (whim-fulfillment) through lawmaking. . . . The people of Europe have watched patiently as one gang after another has strutted across the stage of European history. . . . The so-called European Community is merely the latest in a long line. (ibid., pp. 2498–9)

The Community's claims to empire and to hegemony cannot be denied. It is indeed imperialistic, because it seeks to exercise dominion over constituent communities. The putatively transcendent 'idea' of Europe is its propaganda, and the mechanism for this dominion, as Allott points out, is the law. It enforces the norms which determine the social, political and economic structure that describes the Community. It thus creates the boundaries and the margins of Europe. At the same time, of course, it also excludes, because it describes that which falls outside the law, and outside 'Europe'. This is the power of European law, and it is at this that critique must be directed. The remaining chapters of this book seek to provide such a critique; not 'the' critique of course, but 'a' critique. Above all else the prerequisite to such a critique is a preparedness to be sceptical. Rather than castigating scepticism as somehow being against the moral European grain, we must embrace scepticism for the potential which it enjoys to explore these legal margins and to erase them.

2 A Brief History of Europe

Europe, it seems, was invented in 1957. European law was invented at the same time. It was also invented as an ahistorical idea. As I suggested in the previous chapter, the attempt to deny its history is one of the defining characteristic of our new Europe. European lawyers, it again seems, are more than happy to support this particular mythology. The major texts on European law are almost brazenly ahistorical. Wyatt and Dashwood's *European Community Law*, for example, relinquishes precisely 16 pages out of a total of 690 to the consideration of history (Wyatt & Dashwood, 1993). Weatherill and Beaumont's *EC Law* provides 35 pages of historical commentary out of 846 (Weatherill & Beaumont, 1993). The bigger and more ambitious the tome, the more striking the absence. The most recent contribution to the burgeoning market, Craig & de Burca's *EC Law: Texts, Cases & Materials*, is a magisterial 1160 pages in length. Both the 'history' and the 'ideas' of Europe are covered between pages 2 and 8 (Craig & de Burca, 1995). The historical context of European law is not taken very seriously at all. It would be easy to suggest that this is a mistake. It is not. The absence of a historical context is a direct product of the particular ideological basis of the Community itself. As I suggested in the previous chapter, the new Europe complements an ideology which aspires to the end of history, and then to go beyond it. Its universal aspirations render history both unnecessary and dangerous (Laurent, 1989). The purpose of this chapter is to reintroduce a historical context precisely because it is subversive. The history of the Community, and its pre-history, contextualises the ideological pretensions which dictate the margins of European law. At the same time, I also want to present a 'history' of the Community as a positive force. As Anthony Smith has repeatedly emphasised, it is the absence of such a history, and pre-history, which serves to negate the possibility of a 'European' identity ultimately emerging. The 'new' Europe needs the 'old', and the fact that history of the 'old' Europe is actually a history of difference, as Derrida suggests, actually strengthens the identity rather than weakens it. Without a history there cannot be the 'collective memory' which is such an integral part of identity creation (Smith, 1992). Aspects of this 'history' will be emphasised in the first three sections of this chapter. In the final section, I shall then concentrate on certain of the resultant contradictions and tensions which have remained at the heart of the new Europe. These tensions can only be understood, and perhaps addressed, in a historical context. It is these tensions, and their effects, which will then be developed in the following chapters of this book.

1 THE ROAD TO ROME

As I intimated in the previous chapter, the 'idea' of Europe is an old one. Various intellectual forefathers can be suggested, ranging from Charlemagne and Hitler to Kant and Nietzsche. But today's Europe is a particularly modern variant on this idea. The more ambitious of legal commentators are prepared to venture back from 1957 and to suggest that the origins of the Community can be seen as early as 1945. The European idea, it seems, sprung up at the end of the Second World War. This is a misconception. The impetus for European union, in its present guise, had already gained an intellectual hold by the end of the First World War. It was this war which convinced everyone that the Bismarckian balance between nation-states no longer ensured peace, even if it could be agreed that it ever had. As Modris Eksteins has graphically portrayed, the old world was indeed breaking up, and with it was going all the political, social and philosophical foundations. The intellectual elites turned to Dhiagalev, Dali and Dadaism, whilst the working class stormed European palaces and executed or exiled their occupants (Eksteins, 1989).

I shall discuss shortly the peculiar ineptitude of successive British governments in Europe, but suffice to say that one of the great ironies of Community history is that the immediate intellectual fuel for its conception was British.

The idea of a European Community, at least in its present twentieth-century, quasi-federal, guise was ours. The British Federal Union was the most vigorous proponent of integration. Monnet acknowledged that his idea of a 'United States of Europe' was founded on the BFU's proposals. Spinelli similarly bore testament to the role of the Union amongst European intellectuals. Significantly, it was economists such as Lionel Robbins and William Beveridge who campaigned most forcefully. In their eyes the virtue of a European union lay in its money-making capacity. It is a reality common to Community history that, despite idealistic rhetoric, the Community has enjoyed widest support and evidenced greatest integrational vigour when it has most clearly appeared to be making the nation-states richer. Perhaps most significantly of all, the core distinguishing characteristic of the Federal Union plans was for the establishment of a European Constitution. The 1939 Draft Constitution, the most sophisticated document published by the Union, was drafted by lawyers, including most notably Ivor Jennings, and was dominated by a determination to ensure the role of law in defining the new Europe (Ransome, 1991). At the same time, implicitly and explicitly, the Union presumed to design a European federal state constituted by nation-states and protective of the nation-state interest.

Throughout this book, and most notably in the following chapter, I want to stress, again and again, the extent to which the Community has been, and still is, moulded by the often very varied ambitions of these nation-states. One of the few assertions that can be made about the new Europe with any confidence is that everyone has seemed to have a different idea about what shape it should take. This, fairly obviously, is why there is such a chronic lack of identity and definition. The most obvious rivalry is between the so-called supranationalists, who popularly seem to include all those from the most ardent federalists to anyone who vaguely supports the idea of supranational institutions, and the intergovernmentalists, who include an equally disparate bunch, ranging from those who wish to see nothing more than a common market to those who wish to seen nothing more, full stop. There was, not surprisingly, a much wider ideological and political battle being fought. Whilst the likes of

Churchill and de Gaulle clung tenaciously to the political idea of the nation-state, the more radical ideas of the British free market liberals were taken on most vigorously by socialist resistance movements in continental Europe. Most famously, Spinelli and Rossi penned their Ventotene Manifesto, whilst imprisoned for anti-fascist activities. The pervasive fear of all the socialist movements was a post-war return to the elitist nation-state system, and the subtle reassertion of closet fascism in the place of overt fascism. The Ventotene Manifesto warned that

> the most privileged classes in the old national systems will attempt, by underhand or violent methods, to dampen the wave of internationalist feelings and passions and will ostentatiously begin to reconstruct the old State institutions. . . . The question which must be resolved first, failing which progress is no more than mere appearance, is the definitive abolition of the division of Europe into national, sovereign States. The collapse of the majority of the States on the Continent under the German steamroller has given the people of Europe a common destiny: either they will submit to Hitler's dominion or, after his fall they will all enter a revolutionary crisis and thus will not find themselves separated by, and entrenched in, solid State structures. Feelings today are already far more disposed than they were in the past to accept a federal reorganisation of Europe. The harsh experience of recent decades has opened the eyes even of those who refused to see, and has matured many circumstances favourable to our ideal. (Weigall & Stirk, 1992, pp. 29–32)

The continuing nature of this political battle can be seen today in the debate surrounding the place of a social policy in the new Europe. I shall discuss this issue later in the chapter.

Churchill, in contrast to the likes of Spinelli, as his famous 1946 Zurich speech revealed, sought to 'regain' for the 'hundreds of millions of toilers' in Europe 'the simple joys and hopes which make live worth living'. A 'kind of United States of Europe' must be built, he suggested, precisely to preempt any threat of social revolution. Churchill wanted the UK, along with the USA and perhaps the Soviet Union, to sponsor a new, and apparently simple, Europe, founded upon the rehabilitation of Germany (ibid., pp. 40–1). The simple Europeans – and Churchill clearly did not include himself as being at all European – seemed, however, to be somewhat less impressed. The newly founded European Union of Federalists' Montreux resolutions, in 1947, emphasised that Europe must found its own destiny and not merely follow the lead of others. It was a matter of 'pride' and 'legitimate independence' (ibid., p. 42). Harold Laski's *Liberty in the Modern State* was republished and became an instant best-seller. In it he declared that the 'principle of national sovereignty has exhausted its usefulness.' Moreover, he emphasised, the demands of modern global economics rendered the nation-state economically untenable as a discrete economic unit.

The ideology of European integration has always lain in the slipstream of immediate economic necessity, and those who have perceived most to be gained have tended to offer loudest support. It was in Germany, the most obviously socialist state in immediate post-war Europe, and the most impoverished, that integrationist and federal idealism was most apparent. Germany's economic reconstruction, as the Social Democrat politician Carlo Schmid suggested, would be far easier if funded by the rest of Europe, as well as the USA (ibid., pp. 48–9). During the 1950s, the most aggressive proponents of further integration, leading to an economic community, were the Dutch. Holland had comfortably the worst trade deficit in Western Europe (Milward, 1992, pp. 185–91). The Schuman Declaration emphasised the raw economic motivation behind integration ideology. It talked of 'de facto solidarity', as opposed to constitutional and ideological nicety (Weigall & Stirk, 1992, pp. 58–9). Interestingly, Chancellor Adenauer of Germany articulated the realisation that the economic future of the nation-state might depend on a partial 'renunciation' of 'sovereignty' (ibid., p. 67). This is a theme to which I shall return repeatedly throughout this book.

Monnet himself remained torn between wanting to effect closer European integration whilst, at the same time, preserving the interest of the nation-state, and so did a number of his fellow European 'saints', including Spaak, Schuman,

Adenauer and de Gasperi (cf. Milward, 1992, pp. 334–5). The attempt to strike this balance has served to occupy European ruling elites throughout this century (Slater, 1982, pp. 80–1). It has continued to elude the architects of the new Europe. The nature of this problem, and its unsatisfactory resolution, were noted by one of the more unlikely, though certainly perceptive, of critics, the Moscow Institute of World Economics and International Relations, which, on the eve of the Rome Treaty, suggested that

> the promoters and signatories of the Treaties of Rome . . . have to pretend that these Treaties do not have a supranational character and that they contain nothing which could threaten the sovereign rights of any state. But the language of the facts tells otherwise. The Treaties establishing the EEC and Euratom provide for the setting up of various controlling organs. The transference to these institutions of certain important competences in the economic, political and military fields will result in the curtailment of the sovereignty of the weaker states; it will inevitably limit the rights of Parliaments of these countries to make important social and national decisions.

The Community, it continued, was established by social and intellectual elites solely for the purpose of bolstering the flagging fortunes of capitalist ideology, the nation-state and themselves. It was, it concluded, the last throw of the dice (Weigall & Stirk, 1992, pp. 109–11; cf. Urwin, 1995, p. 10). Only time will tell if this final prophesy is true.

2 THE PILGRIMS' PROGRESS

The history of the European Community can be told as a history of a pilgrimage. Rather like Bunyan's pilgrim, Christian, the advocates of a 'closer Union' have progressed from one 'slough of Despond' to another, in the increasingly desperate hope that they would stumble across a Celestial City. As the pilgrims arrive, ever more exhausted and desperate, and each Treaty is established, the confusion with regard to what the Community is supposed to be increases. We have three of these Treaties to consider. As the 1950s progressed, and the ECSC seemed to work, the idea of sacrificing a bit of sovereignty for a lot of wealth seemed better and better, and pretty soon everyone wanted to be involved. The Spaak Report suggested that a 'common market' would make everyone a lot of money, and that was all anyone needed to hear. The Treaty of Rome, which established the Common Market, was many things, but most importantly, it was quick. As Stuart Holland has suggested, it was a 'rushed job'. The inevitable result of such expedition was a 'negative' Treaty, stating lots of things which could not be done, but practically nothing with regard to what should be done. To a certain extent this is perhaps endemic to a free trade treaty, even one as unfree as the Treaty of Rome, but such a 'minimalist' approach has acted as a break on the wider interests of European political and social integration (Holland, 1980, p. 10; cf. Williams, 1991, pp. 25–7).

Twenty years after the inception of the Community, the Common Market had hardly progressed at all. The much vaunted functionalist 'spillover' never happened, except in books. As the world recession bit during the 1960s, the 'peoples' of Europe retreated behind the national boundaries. In 1962, de Gaulle caustically observed, 'at present there is and can be no Europe other than a Europe of the states – except, of course, for myths, fictions and pageants' (Holland, 1993, p. 9). Successive oil crises during the 1970s kept the process of integration in abeyance. There were occasional bursts of euphoria, such as that caused by de Gaulle's demise in 1969, and numerous reports, all of which promised jam tomorrow and all of which were ignored by member states intent on enhancing preferential trading positions. The Tindemans Report waxed lyrically on the subject of European integration as a 'self-evident good', and advocated all sorts of wholly unacceptable ideas, such as enhanced democratic accountability, and even more unacceptable measures, such as majority voting in the Council. The Three Wise Men Commission was established in 1979 to examine the failures of the Community, and found plenty.

By the early 1980s, Europe was thoroughly fed up, and so were its peoples. As Derek Urwin suggests, Europe appeared to be simply 'stumbling from suggestion to suggestion' (Urwin, 1995, p. 180). The Community was described by Commissioner

Dankert as a 'feeble cardiac patient'. He seemed disappointed that the member states only proposed further integration when it was clear that there was money to be made in it. What was really lacking, he more perceptively observed, was a distinct European identity, which could itself then appeal for popular support beyond the nation-state (Dankert, 1982). As Martin Slater emphasises, the Community appeared, more than ever, to be a Community run by political and economic elites for political and economic elites (Slater, 1982). The Community responded by setting up the Adonnino Committee to look into the problem of identity. It responded by recommending the immediately vital need to establish an EC radio station, an EC flag, an EC hymn and if possible, an EC space station.

Whilst the crushingly indifferent peoples of Europe were to be thus converted, the more constitutionally ambitious set about reforming the Treaty framework. The impetus for reform came from the Parliament, a delegation from which, headed by Spinelli, drafted a new European Treaty over dinner at the Crocodile restaurant in Strasbourg. Unsurprisingly, the draft Treaty came out strongly in favour of increased parliamentary power. Equally unsurprisingly, it was summarily ignored by the Council (Cardozo & Corbett, 1986; Lodge, 1984, pp. 387–92). As ever, it was the promise of increased economic reward which finally convinced the member states that there might be a virtue in refining the Treaty framework, and moreover it was better that they did it, rather than leave it to the unreliable whimsy of the Parliament. Lord Cockfield famously suggested that a mere 279 measures could realise the idyll of a single internal market. The result was the Single European Act, which included provision for the 279 measures, but only marginally enhanced Parliament's power to delay legislation, and curiously said nothing about either an EC hymn or a space station. Parliament voted down the Treaty, by 243 votes to 47, but the Council ignored it and carried on anyway.

The Single European Act seemed to disappoint everyone, except that is the nation-states who had written it. Pierre Pescatore thought it a 'severe setback' for the cause of integration, which was, of course, precisely what it was intended to be (Pescatore, 1987). As George Bermann perceptively observed, the Single European Act, like the Rome Treaty before it, was very much the result of an attempt to compromise very different rival political visions of Europe. It was the 'product of a careful tempering of integrationalist impulses with preoccupations of national sovereignty' (Bermann, 1984, p. 529). The solution to the particular problems thrown up by the Single Act, as everyone immediately agreed, was another Treaty. This, luckily enough, was provided for anyway by the Single Act, which established the '1992 Project' to effect Cockfield's 279 measure by the end of 1992. The mere establishment of the 1992 totem inspired an almost hysterical euphoria. Before anything had been done to realise it, Commissioner Ehlermann declared the whole thing an 'outstanding success'. It should perhaps be noted that Ehlermann, virtually alone, also thought that the Single Act was 'startlingly successful' (Ehlermann, 1990).

Cunningly sensing the most sensitive nerve of the nation-states, Community institutions issued a whole series of reports suggesting the considerable riches to made by realising a closer Europe. The Cecchini Report notoriously made up all sorts of unlikely figures, which a worryingly large number of people seemed to believe (Wise & Gibb, 1993, p. 101). In rather more sober fashion, the Delors Commission recommended that the Community should be better financed and have more money itself. It also suggested the need for monetary union and a common currency, governed by a European Bank. Politically, the proposal for monetary union and common currency remains hugely contentious, and the inevitable arguments surrounding potential loss of sovereignty have been hot. They have, however, been generally accepted by the member states, with the notable exception of the UK, and it is further evidence that, providing there is real economic gain on offer, there is little that the member states will not sacrifice (Harden, 1990).

Cometh the hour, cometh another Treaty. The pilgrims arrived next at Maastricht. I shall reserve discussion of constitutional implications of the Maastricht Treaty on European Union for the next chapter. Suffice to say they were, once again, to be disappointed. There was little in the Maastricht Treaty which suggested that the boundaries of the new Europe would go any further than those which could be justified by the allure of greater economic prosperity (Urwin, 1995, pp. 255–6). The provisions to enhance economic cohesion were the most substantive, because they were the only ones that really mattered. Articles 102–9 enacted the Delors proposals: an exchange rate mechanism, which almost immediately fell to pieces, a common currency, which has not yet happened, and a Central European Bank. Given the persistent economic disequilibrium between the various member states, Delors recommended a 'two-tier' economic process, with member states able to 'select' the speed at which they wished to engage in currency alignment and union. In reality, numerous convergence criteria were established, which the poorer countries could not hope to meet. There was thus one speed for the more stable economies and currencies, so that they could get richer quickly, and another speed for the less stable, who would get rather less rich, rather less quickly. The extremely rich Germans were the keenest, the extremely poor Italians the least keen (Artis, 1992). In contrast, with regard to non-economic measures, there was, as we shall see in subsequent chapters, merely obfuscation and much confusion; over subsidiarity, over citizenship, over the democratic deficit, over the asylum and immigration procedures, over the status of human rights, over the role of social policy, and so on. As Helen Wallace emphasises, the Maastricht Treaty seemed to reinforce all the essential problems which have beset the Community since its inception, and are, moreover, symptomatic of a wider malaise in modern government:

> technocracy and an elite-driven process seem no longer an adequate basis for EC governance. The gap between governed and governors within and between countries is serious and created havoc in the debate about Maastricht to which technical and legalistic devices seemed an inappropriate response. (Wallace, 1984)

3 THE UK EXPERIENCE OF INTEGRATION

As in all pilgrimages, pilgrims come from different communities and bring different cultures with them.

Jurisprudential pilgrims bring different legal cultures. Pilgrims also enjoy, and then contribute, distinctive experiences. This is no less so of the latterday pilgrimage towards the Holy Grail of an integrated Europe. A brief history of the Community is also a brief history of the nation-states and their individual experiences. It is quite beyond the capacity of this chapter, or book, to present each and every history of each and every member state. It is also unnecessary. Any history is a history written in the particular. The UK experience is such a particular history and such a particular description. Our own history of the European Community – the British history – is, then, rather different from everyone else's. But, as an example of the wider issues of European political integration, it is no less illustrative or instructive for being particular. That is in the nature of history; it is written differently by different interests for particular audiences.

The UK has always seen itself as playing a particular role in the new Europe. As I suggested above, in the very earliest days, the idea of a federal Europe was more popular in the UK than perhaps anywhere else in Europe. Federalism was enormously popular in the UK in the years preceding 1939, not least because it seemed to be the only way of opposing or appeasing Hitler; advocates of both alternatives seemed to think that a federal Europe was the only solution. In 1940, a year after the outbreak of war, Churchill still talked of the 'indissoluble' union between France and the UK as the fulcrum of a new Europe. His deputy prime minister, Clement Attlee, had already asserted that all of 'Europe must federate or perish'. Despite this rhetoric, it is clear that the British role was perceived, at least by the British, to be outside Europe, and it was from the outside that it hoped to provide the lead (Urwin, 1995, p. 31). Unfortunately, this was not a scenario which the rest of Europe, and President de Gaulle in particular, was prepared to countenance (Young, 1993, pp. 9–12).

British governments struggled consistently against any form of supranationalism. Even the Council of Europe, the most intergovernmental of institutions, was seen to be a threat, with Ernest Bevin declaring, somewhat confusedly; 'I don't like it. I don't like it. When you open that Pandora's Box you'll find it full of Trojan Horses' (Greenwood, 1992, p. 30). Despite the support for a new Europe amongst socialist parties on the continent, the British Labour Party joined the Conservatives in their opposition to the idea of the UK becoming part of it. Perversely, the Secretary of State for War, John Strachey, suggested that 'Europeanism' was a dastardly plot to overthrow the Labour Party and the entire socialist movement. He would rather Britain was governed by the Conservative interest than by foreign socialists. Clement Attlee articulated similar fears (Young, 1993, pp. 34, 46). Herbert Morrison decided that Britain could not support the Schuman Plan because the 'Durham miners won't wear it' (George, 1994, p. 20). Moreover, the assumption was that as the Durham miners would not wear it, then the UK could not support it, then it was destined to fail. Belgium, as Alan Milward has emphasised, joined solely to preserve its mining industry. That industry now flourishes (Milward, 1992, pp. 46–118). There are no mines left in Durham. Conservative politicians felt precisely the same way. In 1952 Antony Eden told an audience at Columbia University that joining a European federation was 'something which we know in our bones we cannot do'. The Schuman Plan, he declared, was part of an insidious French plot to 'dominate' Europe (Greenwood, 1992, pp. 42–3; Young, 1993, pp. 29–33). Britain remained on the margins of Europe, occasionally revealing a lukewarm interest, but generally dismissing any notion of transnational affinity. Eden's Chancellor of the Exchequer, R.A. Butler, decided that he was 'bored' with Europe and its 'pushy' foreigners, whilst the Foreign Secretary, Selwyn Lloyd, dismissed the whole European project as 'much ado about nothing' (Greenwood, 1992, pp. 76–7). Eden's successor, Harold Macmillan, declared his dislike of European integration because it was advocated by 'the Jews, the planners and the old cosmopolitan element'. Adenauer he dismissed as 'half mad', whilst de Gaulle, he informed President Kennedy, was attempting to become a new Napoleon (Milward, 1992, p. 432; Young, 1993, pp. 63–4, 69, 83).

Yet Britain eventually joined the Community despite itself. It joined because, in economic terms, it had no choice. Its economic decline had been entrenched by the middle of the nineteenth century. As Sean Greenwood has emphasised, the nature of this decline was crucially paradoxical. On the one hand, it was 'so slow as to be almost imperceptible', whilst at the same time being 'so swift as to baffle reaction' (Greenwood, 1992, p. 1). For nearly three decades after the end of the war, the UK just could not believe that it really would have to join a European Community. Despite Macmillan's xenophobic doubts, the pragmatist in him demanded repeated applications for membership, in 1957 and 1958. The same overtures were repeated by his successor, Harold Wilson. On each occasion they were vetoed by de Gaulle, on the basis that the UK was no longer economically strong enough to be part of the Community. The sterling crisis of 1966 only confirmed this realisation in Wilson's own mind. It also concentrated his determination. Perhaps aptly, it was left to Britain's only true pro-European prime minister, Edward Heath, to oversee entry in 1972 (George, 1994, p. 49). Paradoxically, however, the UK entered just as its economy was recovering from a recession into which the rest of Europe was beginning to fall. The price of the UK's accession was to cushion this fall. It joined, economically, at precisely the wrong time, at precisely the wrong price (Young, 1993, p. 108). Almost immediately, the first oil shock twisted the spiral of world recession. Signalling an attitude which was to become characteristic, the UK immediately declared that it did not feel bound by any common energy policy, and that the North Sea oil reserves were very definitely British and very definitely not European (Greenwood, 1992, pp. 99–100).

Paradoxically perhaps, the only prime minister to make a significant contribution to furthering European integration since 1972 has been Margaret Thatcher. Wilson refused to participate in the referendum over European accession which he had called, though he did dismiss the idea of a Europint, saying that the 'imperial pint is good enough for me and for the British people, and we want it to stay that way' (George, 1994, p. 87). His successor, James Callaghan, conspicuously ignored Europe as much as he could, only attending Council summits in order to be rude to his counterparts from other countries (ibid., p. 99). Yet, whilst Callaghan's Chancellor of the Exchequer, Denis Healey, dismissed the idea of a common currency as 'half-witted', Thatcher waxed lyrically about its values (Young, 1993, pp. 130–5). Her attitude towards Europe was never a principled, or indeed a particularly consistent, one. But perhaps her most important contribution was single-handedly breaking the Luxembourg Accord and the stranglehold of the member states in Council. It was her bloodymindedness over budgetry contributions in 1984, at the Fontainebleau summit, which finally convinced the other member states that there was a need to abandon unanimous voting requirements in Council. It was also Margaret Thatcher who backed President Mitterrand in insisting on Jacques Delors as the new President of the Commission in 1984 (Williams, 1991, pp. 77–8). Thatcher cut a curious figure at the various summits of the 1980s. As one commentator suggests, she appeared to 'rampage from summit to summit as a sort of fishwife Britannia demanding her money back' (Clarke, 1992, p. 15). Chancellor Kohl of Germany adopted the habit of getting up and walking out of summits as soon as Thatcher began to speak. In her notorious Bruges speech, Thatcher railed against the idea of 'some identikit European personality', which sought to impose a socialist European 'super-state', and which, she added for good measure, threatened the spirit of Magna Carta which still, apparently, pervaded British government (Young, 1993, pp. 155–6). On his resignation from her government, Geoffrey Howe made reference to Thatcher's almost neurotic vision of Europe as a 'continent that is positively teeming with ill-intentioned people, scheming in her words, to extinguish democracy' (Greenwood, 1992, p. 116; cf. Alderman & Carter, 1991).

The Thatcher government enjoys the distinction of being the first to be brought down on the issue of Europe. There is a deep irony here. One of the essential problems with the British response to Europe has been the tendency to relegate it behind more immediate domestic issues (Wallace, 1995, pp. 48–50). The European card has been repeatedly used in the cause of often short-term political results. For a while at least, rampaging around European summits and beating up foreigners was a good vote-winner for Margaret Thatcher, or at least so she thought. Unfortunately for her, she had failed to appreciate a sea-change in domestic attitudes, and in her own party. Her anti-European rhetoric became old-fashioned and passé (George, 1994, pp. 162–3, 172–3; Greenwood, 1992, pp. 117–18). Just as Thatcher had forced the appointment of Delors as President of the Commission, so too her successor, John Major, vetoed Delors' putative successor Jean-Luc Dehaene for precisely the same immediate domestic political impact. The European issue continues to haunt Major. The UK's humiliating mismanagement and final withdrawal from the Exchange Rate Mechanism swallowed a quarter of the country's gold reserves and spun the country into an even sharper economic recession. The passage of the Maastricht legislation through Parliament repeatedly threatened to send the Major government the way of his predecessors. As one national newspaper commented, the government seemed to be existing in a state of suspended 'national hysteria' (Ward, 1994a, pp. 77–88). It might fairly be suggested that it still does.

Thatcher's was a blatant scepticism of the most simplified type. For her, the Community represented a threat to the nation-state. To the rest of Europe, it appears to represent the saviour of the nation-state. It is another of the ironies of European politics that both sides want the same thing, but differ fundamentally as to how it can be best achieved. As I shall suggest again in chapter 4, the core of the problem lies with the UK's apparent obsession with sovereignty. Loss of sovereignty seems to threaten a culture which resides deep in our psychology, and which has hidden decades of social and economic crises behind a philosophy of national identity. It is significant that both politicians and members of the public seem more concerned to preserve the visage of the monarch on the national currency than they do in the fundamental questions which surround European policy in such areas as social and human rights. As Stephen George stresses, the problem remains the same: how best to utilise the EC in order to maintain the UK's international interest (George, 1994, p. 40). The UK is no nearer to solving this riddle than it was in 1972 or 1945. Europe and European integration remain an enigma which cannot be avoided or ignored.

Sovereignty remains the political obsession. As Roy Denman has suggested, it encapsulates our 'continuing delusions of grandeur' (Denman, 1995, p. 45). Until it is appreciated that sovereignty and identity alone mean nothing, and that the well-being of the national community can actually be enhanced by relinquishment of sovereignty, then the UK will remain bothered and bewildered, confused and uncertain about its situation in the new European order. The UK is now the fifth poorest country in the Community. It is also comfortably the least democratic in its political structures and most backward with regard to social and human rights (Smith, 1994). There is, thus, much to be gained from deeper integration into Europe, but it does require a correspondingly deeper and more genuine intellectual engagement. It is, unfortunately, highly unlikely that such a debate can be left to our political elite. Such a debate is not in its interest. Indeed, it may be beyond its intellectual capacity. The failure of the UK in Europe is very much the failure of its political elite (Denman, 1995, p. 45). The greatest deceit inflicted on the British people has been the deliberate fashioning of a simplified debate; from Wilson's patronising comments on the Euro-pint to Thatcher's determination to 'bat for Britain' and to 'get our money back'. As Roy Denman has commented, the 'vast majority of children' in the UK 'emerge semi-literate' from an educational experience, and can only find 'solace . . . in the rollicking Europhobia of the two-syllable tabloid press' (ibid.). If the art of government is, as Johnson suggested, to keep the populace in educated ignorance, then we in the UK are strikingly well governed in matters pertaining to Europe.

4 TENSIONS AT THE HEART OF EUROPE

The history of the Community, and the particular history and experience of integration, provides a context for the current tensions which beset the new Europe. I want to introduce four such areas of particular tension in the European Community, all of which are, unsurprisingly, closely related. First, there is the continuing role of the nation-state in a putatively transnational organisation. I shall concentrate further on this particular contradiction in the next chapter. Second, there is the resultant institutional and structural confusion. Monnet was a great believer in institutions, famously commenting, 'only institutions grow wiser; they accumulate collective experience' (Monnet, 1978, p. 393). Yet, in many ways, the real history of the Community can be mapped as a history of inter-institutional rivalry. Article 4 of the Rome Treaty established four main institutions: the Commission, the Council, the Parliament and the Court of Justice. Notoriously, the Parliament has remained strikingly emasculated, prompting complaints of so-called 'democratic deficit'. We shall consider the vacuity of such accusations in chapter 5. As we have already noted, during the 1980s and 1990s, the Parliament has repeatedly attempted to empower itself. Repeatedly, its ambitions have been largely thwarted: in the draft Treaty, the Single European Act and in the Treaty on European Union. Parliament's ambitions were contemptuously ignored by the Council in the Single European Act. The fact that two of the most powerful negotiators, Germany and the UK, were implacably opposed to enhanced democratic accountability was itself sufficient to condemn any such hopes (Bieber et al., 1986, p. 767). The Maastricht Treaty on European Union has done little to alter the balance of power. Institutional reform extends as far as completion of the market requires, and no further. At the end of the day, in the new democratic European Union, the only governmental institution which cannot adopt regulations, directives or decisions on its own is the Parliament (Hartley, 1993, p. 222).

Since the very earliest days, the real power has lain with the Council (Weiler, 1991a, p. 2423). The Council is the most obviously intergovernmental institution, and whilst it has continued to exercise greatest control, the Community has remained essentially intergovernmental. The centre of the Council's power lies in the extent of its veto. As the veto has been eroded so has its power; but only fractionally. The veto was written into the Treaty at the insistence of the French and, enshrined in the Luxembourg Accord, has continued to cripple the integrationist impulse ever since (Weiler, 1991a, pp. 2423–4; Nicoll, 1984). During the 1980s, as the Community sought to reinvigorate the process of integration, there was much talk of the need to enhance the power of the Commission as a counter to the Council.

The problem with government by Council, as Eric Stein observed, was 'that at times its ringing declarations end up in a way reminiscent of the Emperor's orders in Gilbert and Sullivan's *Mikado.* When the Emperor orders something to be done, it is as good as done and therefore, need not be done' (Stein, 1983, pp. 648–9). There is much rhetoric in Council, but little action. This situation is set to continue for so long as the nation-states continue to maintain their predominance in the European political scene. The speed of European integration, and the ambitions of the other institutions, the Commission and the Parliament, remain subject to the overriding demands of the Council.

Lawyers have always tended to support the idea that the real integrational impulse has come from the Court. European Court judges, such as Federico Mancini, are only too keen to suggest that the real European constitution is actually the product of European case law, rather than the Treaties (Mancini, 1991, p. 177). Certainly, there is widespread support for the view that the Court has emerged as the most substantively supranational institution of all. According to Hjalte Rasmussen, 'the Court has successfully acted as an unequivocal and indefatigable promoter of centralism, uniformity and unification.' As Rasmussen has emphasised, the role of the Court in the construction of the new Europe has not been unambiguously straightforward (Rasmussen, 1986, p. 377). Constitutional courts in France, Germany and Italy have all, at times, rejected the jurisdiction of European law and of the Court (Schermers, 1990; Hilf, 1983; Tatham, 1991). During the 1980s, as everyone sought a solution to the apparent demise of European integration, the lawyers, as ever, advocated greater power to the law, meaning themselves (Mancini, 1991, pp. 183–4, 189). In contrast, critics such as Mary Volcansek have castigated an 'arrogance' of the Court, which is only bested by the complacency of its jurisprudential critics. 'What is truly remarkable', she suggests, 'is the almost total lack of criticism and virtual sycophantic praise of the court's actions.' What has really characterised the Court's policy-making, aside from its appeasement of the Council, has been a determination to support the Commission in its struggle to maintain legislative authority over that of the increasingly agitated Parliament

(Volcansek, 1992). As we shall see in chapter 8, the Court has attracted particular criticism with regard to its less than convincing attempt to establish a human rights jurisprudence in European law, in the light of the overt disapproval of certain member states, and implicitly the Council.

The institutional tensions are very much a product of political compromise enunciated in the Treaty framework. The third set of tensions, articulated in the economic provisions of Community law, are more deep-rooted. The free market ideology which lay behind the common market has been torn by a series of tensions and contradictions since its very inception. One of the most striking contradictions established in the Rome Treaty itself was between the desire to promote free trade as a means to overall wealth creation, whilst at the same time effecting economic equilibrium between member states. The clearest example of non-free trade in free trade Europe is agriculture, the peculiar provisions for which were once again written into the Treaty at the insistence of the French. Articles 34–87 are wholly inconsistent with any ethic of free trade (Williams, 1981, pp. 41–2, 118–23). During the first two and half decades of the Community, the Common Agricultural Policy took up 80 per cent of the administrative effort and 70 per cent of the budget of the Community. Vast subsidies led to vast surpluses. Community agricultural policy has become shrouded in myth. One such is the myth of the 'blooming peasant'. Just as the peasantry fuelled the idea of a Merrie England of years gone by, such that Thomas Hardy, at the turn of the century, could look back longingly on the loss of an idyllic era, when in fact life had been impoverished, disease-ridden and squalid, so too the Community became burdened with this myth of the 'blooming peasant', certainly not impoverished or particularly unhealthy, but very, very expensive. The farmer became a protected species, kept in a permanently rarefied atmosphere. If the farmer became extinct, then Rome would truly fall. The collateral myth, fuelled vigorously by Monnet, was that the Community was synonymous with the CAP. Supporting the economically underdeveloped regions of Europe represented all that was best in the 'moral' idea of Europe. More importantly, perhaps, it represented the one genuinely proactive supranational economic policy in the common market (Urwin, 1995, p. 135). As Milward observes, the CAP still lumbers on 'like some clumsy prehistoric mastodon, incapable of evolution into the present world where the political influence of agriculture on parliamentary systems is small indeed, an awesome reminder of the strength which integration could add to the rescue of the nation state' (Milward, 1992, pp. 306–17).

Agriculture is not, of course, the only tension at the heart of Community economic ideology. As we shall see again in the next chapter, the competition law of the Community is riven by contradictions necessitated by the need to accommodate particular national interests. There should not, of course, need to be a 'law' of competition. Pure competition should work without regulation. However, the very idea of a free market founded on pure competition has itself proved to be illusory in practice. The Rome Treaty loudly spoke the language of neo-classical liberal capitalism. Hallstein suggested that the Community would march in the spirit of Adam Smith. But, in truth, there was already a fundamental compromise at the heart of the new Europe. The fulcrum philosophy of free trade was inexorably compromised by the political realities of regulation. Hallstein referred to it as 'regulated competition' (Holland, 1980, p. 4). Article 2 of the Treaty referred to 'harmonious development' and a 'balanced expansion'. But in reality there was little in the Treaty to effect such ambitions. Much faith was placed in 'market mechanisms'. As we have already noted, the Treaty was preventative in nature. It sought to construct little, and as Tsoukalis stresses, what it really articulated was the lowest common denominators of the various nation-state interests. These interests prevented any of the macroeconomic coordination which was so obviously necessary if the grandiose rhetoric of Article 2 was to be realised. Most importantly, according to Tsoukalis, 'the treaty made virtually no provision for redistributive instruments of policy' (Tsoukalis, 1991, p. 19). Economic policy remained firmly in the hands of the nation-states. The dominant economic ideology across much of Europe was Keynesian, and so the primary responsibility for economic management lay with the national governments. Europe moved closer together, but it did so in separate economic units. The nation-state interests demanded regulation and protection. This attitude became ever more apparent during periods of economic recession, as in the 1970s, with the burgeoning of non-tariff barriers, ranging from spurious regulations to effect technical or tax harmonisation to blatant state aids. In 1981, the Commissioner for Industry, Etienne Davignon, feared that such nation-state 'activism' had 'become a veritable challenge to the Community' (ibid., p. 39).

Critics such as Stuart Holland have gone further and suggested that the ideology of the free market is itself contradictory. A free market, in order to work, must be regulated. According to Holland, integration is a capitalist idea, although the conventional theory of integration seeks to deny this. The key result of this denial is an unrealised presumption of a harmony of interests between capital and labour (Holland, 1980, p. 49). This harmony was not 'constructed' by the Rome Treaty, yet even the most confirmed liberal free marketeer recognises that there must be a degree of macroeconomic management of any political economy, and the most immediate management must address the accommodation of capital and labour interests. In the absence of the necessary macroeconomic approach to regulating the market, there is a multitude of microeconomic regulations, in the Community's case, emanating from the nation-states. The result of this, in turn, is the vast disequilibrium in wealth, from one member state to another, and from one region to another (Holland, 1980, pp. 50–8). This, as Joanne Scott has recently emphasised, is a problem which is increasing, rather than decreasing, in today's Community (Scott, 1995). The rich are getting richer, the poor are getting poorer. Writing in 1980, and articulating the particularly acute sense of disillusionment of the time, Holland concluded:

> The failure of economic union and positive integration, in this sense, is not merely an accident of botched institutions or a failure of will in leadership elites. It reflects the basic dominance of economics over politics in a capitalist system, and the key interest of a capitalist class in maintaining its prerogatives over the rest of us. (Holland, 1980, p. 113)

It was this policy vacuum, of course, which the Cockfield Report set out to address. The Report stressed the need for macroeconomic regulation of the free market, concluding:

> Europe stands at the crossroads. We either go ahead – with resolution and determination – or we drop back into mediocrity. We can now either resolve to complete the integration of the economies of Europe; or through a lack of political will to face the immense problems involved, we can simply allow Europe to develop into no more than a free trade area. (Cockfield, 1990, pp. 4–5)

The Common Market, it seemed, had to be more than just a common market. Competition was to be intensified, but, as a number of commentators have noted, it was a very particular type of competition. It was not the 'pure' competition of neo-classical liberalism, but rather the 'workable' competition, with a market structured to favour the oligopolistic interests of companies. The wave of mergers and acquisitions which followed the Single Act – in excess of a 400 per cent increase by the end of the 1980s – reinforced the suspicion that the market was indeed loaded. The stronger companies were seen to gobble up the weaker with striking ease, and as Holland had predicted at the beginning of the decade, such a form of competition merely opened up the market to the powerful, essentially non-European, multinational interests (Tsoukalis, 1991, p. 79). Only with the Delors Commission's determination to realise a common monetary policy can there really be said to be a macroeconomic impulse in Community economic strategy. It finally recognises the futility of a free market approach. As Tsoukalis emphasises, the economic history of the Community during the 1980s and the early 1990s reveals the immanent contradiction in free market ideology, both in theory and, most importantly, in practice (Tsoukalis, 1991, pp. 295–309).

This is a conclusion supported by Stuart Holland in his more recent review of the Community's economic strategy. What is still lacking in the new Europe, after Maastricht more than ever, is positive economic integration. Measures such as monetary union are one solution, but the necessary complementary solution is for a recognition that economic integration must be complemented by social and regional integration (Holland, 1993). This introduces the fourth and final set of tensions embedded in the structure of the Community and its history: the uneasy situation of social policy. Social policy, requiring, as it does, a greater degree of market regulation, has emerged as one of the most contentious issues in contemporary Community politics (Moxon-Browne, 1993, p. 142). The idea of a comprehensive social policy had bounced around in the Community since the early 1970s, but never seemed likely to win sufficient support from all the nation-states. It is no coincidence that the poorest countries, such as Portugal and Italy, have been amongst the most positive, whilst the richest, such as Germany and the UK, have been more negative (George, 1991, p. 194). Yet, with the determination to intensify European integration during the mid-1980s, the issue of social policy again returned to the fore. Certain issues of pressing concern with regard to social policy will be considered in subsequent chapters, most notably the rights of non-EC nationals, sex equality and human rights. The ambivalent situation of these issues in the new Europe is very much a result of the dominance of economic imperatives over the social in the history and development of the Community.

Aside from these immediate examples, the overriding ambition of those who favour a social 'face' in the new Europe is for a 'social dialogue'. According to Paul Teague, such a dialogue would represent an 'opportunity structure' which could encapsulate the 'ideological principles of social cooperation and consensus' (Teague, 1989, pp. 108–11). The idea of such a dialogue has become a centrepiece of Commission rhetoric. Yet it is instructive that such a dialogue is taken to mean a dialogue between economic interests and economic actors. The Marin and then the Papandreou Reports both referred to the need for the Community to project itself as being a community for everyone, not just for businesspeople. Yet, the resultant Charter for the Social Rights of Workers, was precisely that: a document – ultimately toothless – which talked about rights for those in employment, who happened to be registered nationals of the member states (Lodge, 1990, pp. 137–41, 149–50). The general exasperation with regard to the so-called 'social dialogue' was articulated by an Irish MEP, de Rossa, who accused the member states of a cruel deceit: 'Few issues have generated as much hypocrisy as this one has. From the outset it has been used as a placebo to placate workers and their representatives and lead them to believe that they were not left behind in the drive towards the single market' (Wise & Gibb, 1993, p. 178).

The Maastricht Treaty has only served to confuse the situation, by adding an Agreement on Social Policy, which can be approved by qualified majority voting, to the existing rather scanty bases for social policy legislation in the Rome Treaty and Single Act, which still requires unanimity. As Erika Szyszcak has observed, after Maastricht, 'Social policy, so long the Cinderella of the common market, has been transformed, not into a fairy princess, but into an ugly sister of the internal market.' The shattering of the legal base, she adds, has 'called into question the future of the European integration process' (Szyszczak, 1994, p. 313). The politics of the Maastricht Agreement and Protocol serves only to underline the yawning abyss which seems to lie between the rival aspirations, of internal market deregulation and social policy regulation. To date there can be little doubt that the free market ideologues have emerged ahead in the ensuing struggle. But, as we shall see in chapter 5, the increasing interest in redefining alternative forms of citizenship, along social as opposed to purely political lines, may yet signal a new impetus towards a social Europe. It should be impressed that such a solution may be the only viable and immediate way of redressing the deep social scars which disfigure a Europe in which one in six are designated by the Commission to be officially 'poor'. The ratio is all the greater in the poorer countries, such as Eire, Greece, Portugal and Spain, together with the UK, where social policy has been consistently neglected, and where disparities in wealth are greater than in any other member state. The Second European Poverty Programme concluded that, in light of these conclusions:

> There is a considerable risk of two different societies developing within the Member States, one of them active, well-paid, well-protected socially, and with an employment-conditioned structure; the other poor, deprived of rights and devalued by inactivity. (Holland, 1993, p. 125)

This is the Europe that we have constructed so far and, I would suggest, it is the Europe that that we are continuing to construct today. The following chapters of this book will seek to underline the discrepancies and deceits of the new Europe, its inconsistencies and downright injustices. They will also seek to present alternatives; reconstruction as well as deconstruction. But as each chapter discusses a different perspective, it is important to remember the historicity of the debate. The new Europe is very much a product of the old, of its ideology and its prejudices. It is a Community which appears to desire a supranational identity, but which exists, as we shall see in the next chapter, primarily to preserve the nation-state. It is a Europe built to make money, but which merely serves to divert it. It is a Europe founded upon an economic ideology which requires exploitation and marginalisation. It is a Europe of winners and losers, in a game refereed by its lawyers and its judges.

Part II

The Limits of Constitutionalism

3 The Myth of Integration

In this chapter I want to concentrate on another particular sceptical critique. I want to suggest that the whole idea of European integration is a myth, a 'cruel deceit'. The nation-states have never really intended that there should be anything more than a kind of asymptotic process of integration; the appearance that integration was getting closer and closer, but the reality that any ultimate integration would remain unrealised and unrealisable. There have always been limits to integration, limits which have varied from one nation-state to another. To develop this thesis I want to introduce yet another sceptical voice in European studies, that of Alan Milward. I shall develop his thesis in the second section of this chapter, but first I want to discuss some of the constitutional tensions which seem to pervade the new Europe. The expressions of confusion and dismay which so characterise current legal writing in the wake of the Maastricht Treaty, I shall suggest, can only be properly understood in the light of a sceptical thesis which properly stresses that the power in the new Union lies as much as ever, indeed even more so, with the nation-states.

1 CONSTITUTIONAL TENSIONS

For most lawyers, it seems fair to say, the Maastricht Treaty has proved to be something of a disappointment. The frustration at the perceived inadequacies of the Rome Treaty and the Single European Act to effect a concrete constitutional foundation for the Communities seems to have been exacerbated. Rather than resolving these frustrations, Maastricht merely serves to emphasise them. Ulrich Everling regrets the ambiguities which pervade the texts, and concludes that at best the constitutional structure of the new Union is 'rudimentary' (Everling, 1992). According to Deidre Curtin, the final Treaty document 'reveals more of a bricoleur's amateurism than a master-bricklayer's strive for perfection and detail'. She concludes scathingly:

> The result of the Maastricht summit is an umbrella Union threatening to lead to constitutional chaos; the potential victims are the cohesiveness and the unity and the concomitant power of a legal system painstakingly constructed over the course of some 30 odd years. And yet the European Parliament and the national parliaments (and the people in three member states) are presented with this *fait accompli* and bullied into believing that only 'bad Europeans' would reject it . . . It must be said, at the heart of all this chaos and fragmentation, the unique *sui generis* nature of the European Community, its true world-historical significance, is being destroyed. (Curtin, 1993, p. 67)

To a certain extent, perhaps, this disappointment was all the greater because of the over-optimism which had accompanied its expectation. As we have already seen in the previous chapter, the Single European Act had proved to be as big a disappointment as the Maastricht Treaty is now. Juliet Lodge called the Act a 'retrograde move' (Lodge, 1986, p. 221). Pierre Pescatore suggested that, 'Putting into force the Single Act would . . . mark a severe setback for the European Community. I am among those who think that forgetting about the Single Act would be a lesser evil for our common future than ratification of this diplomatic document.' He concluded that the 'lip-service paid . . . to the "European idea" is no substitute for real progress towards democracy and political cooperation' (Pescatore, 1987, pp. 17–18). But rather than taking heed of its fate, everyone merely intensified their optimism around the one enduring legacy of the Single European Act, the '1992 Project', which was intended to effect the completion of the internal market by the end of 1992. In doing so it was supposed to realise the various ambitions that lay behind Lord Cockfield's White Paper, which had suggested 279 measures for completing this market. Although it established little itself, in announcing the Project, the Single European Act presented an icon. If there was no jam today, plenty was promised for tomorrow. Claus Ehlermann assured everyone that the Project, as it would be concluded in the Maastricht Treaty, would effect the 'most ambitious and successful legislative program ever adopted by the Community'. It was all proving to be an 'outstanding success' (Ehlermann, 1990). The publication of the Cecchini Report in 1988 added a degree of urgency to the mounting hysteria. The Community, it concluded, was wasting money, in considerable amounts, and much, it promised, could be saved by the completion of the internal market which the Project promised. The implication of greater constitutional consistency was carried along with a more immediate assurance that everyone would be richer (Dehousse, 1988, p. 117; Wise & Gibb, 1993, p. 101). This, moreover, remained the consistent assurance of the Delors Commission, which provided a continuing impetus for the Project.

Implicit in the determination to intensify the process of economic and political integration is the accusation that the current constitutional framework, as prescribed by the Treaties, is now inadequate. To an extent, this has always been the case. The Treaties provide only the barest of skeletons, and the flesh of the European constitution has been nourished by the European Court of Justice and the development of various now-familiar legal principles, such as supremacy and direct effect. The politicians have tacitly approved this proactive constitutionalism. For some commentators, such as Bengoetxea, this is one of the great strengths of the European constitution (Bengoetxea, 1993). For others, most obviously perhaps Rasmussen, writing in the mid-1980s, the approval is more akin to a sin of omission. According to Rasmussen, the Court was 'running wild', consciously abusing its constitutionally defined role in an attempt to force political integration via jurisprudential means (Rasmussen, 1986). Either way, it is clear that the Court has been in the vanguard of legal integration, and thus political integration, and, moreover, public law has perhaps been at the vanguard of the vanguard. The European constitution, it was clear, was something more than the Treaty framework, which, by implication, was no longer sufficient or appropriate for the ambitions of the new Europe.

This was the ambition which appeared to lie behind the new European Union; to consolidate and to redefine. The weary, but elated, pilgrims, having proved their worth by their commitment to the Project, were to arrive at the Celestial City of Maastricht, where they would joyously celebrate the completion of the internal market, give due praise to the Delors Commission and wait for the manna to drop. Unfortunately, this was not to be. There were, of course, the usual rather aimless platitudes in the Preamble, which were then followed by the Common Provisions, Article A of which set off grandly enough, declaring that the newly renamed Union, even if it was no longer intended to harbour overtly federal ambitions, still represents 'a new stage in the process of creating an ever closer union among the peoples of Europe, in which decisions are taken as closely as possible to the people'. Perhaps more instructive, as least in so far as vacuous platitudes go, was Article F, which promised that the Union would 'respect the national identities of its Member States, whose systems of government are founded on the principles of democracy'. Unfortunately, as far as remodelling the constitution goes, that was about it. There was, of course, the three pillars structure. The existing constitution, which, encapsulated in the newly presented idea of Community citizenship, established the first pillar, was to be complemented by two further pillars: common foreign and security policy, and justice and home affairs. The new Union thus supplements the existing Community, but does so, rather incoherently, under one constitutional order. Two words, it seems, Community and Union, but one ambition. As if to set a trend for the rest of the Treaty, there was no definition of what either 'justice' or 'home affairs' actually meant, although this perhaps mattered less given that the 'common interests' supposed to be covered by justice and home affairs were limited to nine areas of marginal impact, with a preponderance addressing issues of asylum and border controls (Mueller-Graff, 1994).

The best, and most obvious, example of the ambiguity which characterised the Maastricht Treaty, and which caused such disappointment, is subsidiarity. Legal reaction has varied from the perplexed to the hostile. The counterpoising of a substantive definition of subsidiarity in Article A, with a contradictory procedural alternative in Article 3B, which establishes the parameters of exclusive competence in such a manner as to defend the nation-state interest, has been dismissed as a 'nonsense' (Peterson, 1994). The matter is not helped by the uncertain status of Article A. Only Article

3B is obviously justiciable as part of the amended Rome Treaty. It may be that Article A is not actually part of constitutional law at all. This is a conclusion reached by Coppel, who adds that the deliberate counterpoising of the two 'definitions' of subsidiarity 'put in place a formulation which is, at best confusing and at worst incoherent' (Coppel, 1993). It is certainly far from clear from the position of constitutional law whether Article 3B suggests a centralising or decentralising definition. Some commentators plump for the former, others for the latter (Toth, 1994; cf. Emiliou, 1994).

Other commentators, in contrast, have seemed rather more resigned to the situation. At least the reasons for it seem to be better understood. Although presented as the fulcrum of the new European constitution, subsidiarity is a political concept taken by the politicians to be the 'glue' by which they could cobble together a political compromise. It prevented, as Peterson has suggested, the entire Treaty from coming 'unstuck' (Peterson, 1994, p. 121). Subsidiarity was never intended to be clear and concise. Indeed, its purpose was quite the opposite. Subsidiarity was an immediate response to an immediate political situation. Lord Mackenzie Stuart, whilst asserting the jurisprudential desirability of a precise definition, recognised that it was quite clear from the preceding Intergovernmental Conferences (IGCs), that the member states saw subsidiarity as a means of appearing to effect the impossible. It was never intended to be more than a mere 'prophylactic' against the vexed question of the ceding of sovereignty (Mackenzie Stuart, 1992). Anthony Teasdale has similarly suggested that the great virtue of subsidiarity was that, paradoxically, it 'satisfied nobody completely' (Teasdale, 1993, pp. 189–91).

The net effect of the political compromise which determined subsidiarity is a concept, and thus a constitutional order, which can mean anything to anybody (Coppel, 1993). For those, the majority perhaps, who had wanted the Treaty expressly to establish a common federal ambition, as was stated in the Dutch draft of the Treaty, subsidiarity was a consolation. In the true spirit of Community political rhetoric it promised something for the future which it was unable to deliver in the present. Subsidiarity is one more step, they were assured, towards the federal goal. It certainly enjoys that connotation in the German constitution. As Ruud Lubbers commented, 'I respect subsidiarity. As you know, for the Germans, the word for this is federalism.' Yet, at the same time, for those who feared the emergence of a federal Union, subsidiarity could be a reassurance against federalism. Thus John Major was able to return from Maastricht and triumph subsidiarity as a step away from a federal Europe. The European constitution thus remains somewhat ill-defined and underdeveloped. It is clearly something more, at least in practice, than what is stated in the rhetoric of the Treaty framework. Yet, at the same time as the European Court has reined back from its earlier, more aggressive integrational impulses, the constitutional vacuum appears all the greater. It remains ill-defined simply because there remains a residual political uncertainty as to how the new Union should be determined. This is not to mean that the individual member states are uncertain. Everyone has their own opinions. The problem is that there is a corporate uncertainty.

2 THE 'RESCUE' OF THE NATION-STATE

It is Alan Milward's thesis that the member states have never seriously contemplated a genuine European constitution. That is why no such thing actually exists and why the European Court has been forced to create the fiction that the Treaty framework somehow actually represents a constitutional document. The problem with European integration studies, he suggests, is that everyone is taken in by the Community's ideological rhetoric. The Community is not the 'antithesis' of the nation-state. Indeed the contrary is true. The sole purpose of the Community is to buttress the nation-state. The 'evolution' of the Community, he suggests, 'has been an integral part of the reassertion of the nation-state as an organizational concept' (Milward, 1992, pp. 2–3). The individual nation-states after 1945 established a Community, according to Milward, because that was the only perceived way of preserving the concept of nation-statehood. The Community was, thus, established precisely to avoid any threat to the nation-state, and as a counter against either dissolution into fragmentary communities or the emergence of a supranational Europe. Recognition of this necessity was implicit in the functionalist theories of such as Haas and Lindberg, which were so popular during the early years of the Community. It was clear, in the years immediately following 1945, that the nation-states could no longer 'function' in isolation (ibid., pp. 8–19).

It is a central theme of Milward's thesis that the ideological rhetoric of integration is a deliberate smokescreen thrown up by the Community to mask these very practical and immediate political motives. The critical commodity in post-war European economic policy, according to Milward, was coal. By way of an example, Milward presents a case-study of the Belgian coal industry. National management dictated the Belgian response to the proposed formation of a European Community. In the post-war years the Belgian government adopted a highly protectionist policy towards its coal industry. Despite its often articulated doubts with regard to Monnet's idealism, and even greater doubts about the suitability or desirability of a European community of nations, the Belgian government entered the European Coal, Iron and Steel Community solely so that it could maintain its pricing policy against the threat of cheaper German coal. In fact, the Belgian coal industry continued to flounder throughout the later 1950s, but without the ECSC protection it would probably have totally disintegrated (ibid., pp. 46–118). If coal was the critical commodity, the critical nation was Germany. The future of Europe after 1945 depended upon German 'prosperity'. If the German nation-state could regain its national economic strength, then so, it was generally perceived, the rest of the nation-states would regain theirs. During the 1950s Germany was the dominant source of both imports and exports throughout Western Europe. There were two essential strengths in the German economy. First, as the British Board of Trade reported in 1956, Germany was better protected against competition than any other nation-state, and second, it concentrated on the manufacture of investment goods, such as machinery, steel and engineering. The German success made the need to develop a European economy policy around it more and more pressing. Most importantly, Germany needed to be 'bound in place' by a series of economic agreements (ibid., pp. 118–67).

The original intent of the Community's founders, Milward suggests, can then be perceived in the establishment of the European Coal and Steel Community. Its essential purpose was precisely to effect the 'binding' of Germany 'in place'. The two leading players, France and Germany, both saw the association as the only way of maintaining their individual economic hegemony in their respective agricultural and coal and steel sectors (ibid., p. 14). Famously, France only acceded to the ECSC and later the European Economic Community when its particular agricultural interest was guaranteed in the Treaty frameworks. The idea of joining a Community could only be sold to the French people, as Faure acknowledged, if it could be clearly shown that it was in the immediate economic interests of the French nation (ibid., pp. 208–16). The continuation of the Common Agricultural Policy is the most eloquent testimony to the determination of the founders of the Community to maintain their individual national interests. If coal and steel were the dominant commodities during the 1950s and early 1960s, it was agriculture which emerged to dominate the following two decades. Agriculture has always been associated with national interests. There was, as Milward suggests, a peculiar ideology of national agriculture, associated with the myth of the 'blooming peasant'. A nation's agriculture was somehow seen as representing its economic soul. Nowhere was this myth stronger than in France. Indeed, as suggested, France joined the ESCS and the Community, not because of any European ideal, but because it was the only way in which it, as a nation-state, could fulfil the fantasies of its own 'blooming' farmers. If the ESCS was an agreement which could found French agriculture on the strength of the German Deutschmark, the CAP, in retrospect, can be seen as nothing more than a 'agricultural trade bargain', designed to preserve for a little longer the myth that French and Dutch agriculture in particular was somehow competitive with German industry (ibid., pp. 224–317).

It was the apparent success of the ECSC and the Community in securing the economic interests of the nation-states, in the early years, which ensured their survival. Success bred success. It did indeed seem to be the case that the economic restructuring which was required in post-war Europe could be better effected by a degree of controlled interdependence. A collateral argument here is that the economic growth which characterised the years 1945–68 was not then solely the product of greater Community interdependence, but was rather as much the result of more effective nation-state economic management, facilitated by the Community's role in strengthening the nation-states' hands. Rather than declining, the extent of national economic management actually increased, most spectacularly perhaps in France (ibid., pp. 21–45). Other nation-states gravitated around the ECSC, and became increasingly convinced that their best interests were served by joining a European economic community, purely because of this perceived success in the early years. Belgium was, of course, one. Another was the Netherlands. During the 1950s it consistently suffered the worst balance of payments deficit in Western Europe. The Dutch foreign minister, Beyen, became the most active advocate of a European economic community. It was Beyen's proposals which were taken on by Monnet and Spaak at the Messina Conference (ibid., pp. 173–96). Ultimately, then, what Milward is really emphasising is that the origins of the Community, and the Community's constitutional framework, the Treaty of Rome, was never intended to realise the rhetorical ambitions of those he terms the European 'saints', such as Monnet or Spaak. The Treaty was effected by backstairs political jobbing and a great deal of 'undignified trading'. The Treaty was cast as precisely such a political expedient, and so, as Milward suggests, the new constitutional framework was always intended to be subservient to, and limited by, the nation-states (ibid., pp. 222–3).

The role of these 'saints' is one of the most challenging and persuasive of Milward's arguments. The 'historiography' of Europe, he asserts, is 'dominated by the legends of great men'. It was these men, most obviously such as Monnet and Spaak, who recognised the threat to the nation-state after 1945, and who set about to preserve it. Spaak, for example, who emerged from the Messina Conference as the most articulate ideologue, was concerned not with establishing any sort of free trade Europe, but primarily with setting up a minimalist customs union in an effort to preserve the internal and external security of the Western European nation-states. His 'ideology' was, in fact, one of 'pragmatism . . . increasingly tainted with utopianism and then with cynicism' (ibid., p. 319). Another who only converted to the idea of European integration once it became clear that it was the only viable way of preserving the nation-state was Robert Schuman. The nation-state remained as the 'basis of his political thought'. Revealingly, whilst drafting his famous Declaration, Schuman confirmed that: 'Our European States are a historical reality; it would be psychologically impossible to make them disappear. Their diversity is in fact very fortunate and we do not want either to level them or to equalize them.' Supranational institutions, he continued, were merely of 'technical' value, and were not intended to affect in any way the 'functions' of nation-state 'sovereignty' (ibid., pp. 325–9). One of the most striking characteristics of these 'saints' – Spaak, Schuman, Adenauer, de Gasperi, Monnet – is their common Catholic affinity. That their political visions should be framed by a corresponding catholicity is then no surprise. The 'archangel' of the European 'saints' is, of course, Jean Monnet. Monnet's politics was more nation-state oriented than any of the others. It was also less democratic. The fact that the Treaty of Rome made only the barest of gestures towards democratic accountability can be traced to Monnet's influence. Community democracy was the clearest threat to the hegemony of the nation-states, and it was thus completely marginalised in Monnet's own vision for Europe. Monnet remained a fervent supporter of the French nation-state, and the wider European interest always remained subservient to it (ibid., pp. 334–7).

Taken in this context, then, the attitude of the UK towards Europe, both in the past and the present, is not at all surprising. Like everyone else, the UK entered the Community purely to preserve its national interest, and the European debate in the UK, ever since the earliest days, has remained very much concentrated on raw nationalistic lines. It was during the 1950s that the weakness of the British position, both economically and politically, became clear. British industry, as Milward notes, had been in a state of consistent decline ever since the late nineteenth century, and by the middle of this century it was plain for all to see. The rise and rise of German industry merely emphasised the threat. The 'car wars' were a prime example. The UK invested millions in supporting its car industry, almost as a last stand against Germany. But by 1956, German car production was outstripping the UK's, and the gap widened as each year progressed to the end of the decade (ibid., pp. 346–66, 395–433). It has been commonplace in recent years to castigate the UK for seeming to place the national interest above the European. In reality, it is not the actual primacy of the national interest which distinguishes the UK's position. Its attitude is precisely in line with that of the rest of the member states. It is the brazenness of the attitude which is striking. UK governments, particularly during the 1980s, made no pretence of championing anything else but the national interest. The UK did not play the game as well as its member states, and by failing to pay lip-service to the rhetoric of European ideology, it found itself castigated as an ideological leper. Milward concludes his thesis by emphasising that, just as the arguments and ambitions of the UK government are thus the same now as they were in the 1950s, the same is true of all the member states. The Community exists, still, purely and simply to 'rescue' the nation-state. The Maastricht Treaty, as he emphasises, is no nearer towards actually establishing a European 'state' than it was in the 1950s, and it is no nearer because a European state is not in the interests of any of the member nation-states. There is no common currency, no genuinely democratic, empowered or organised European Parliament, no accountable executive and, as yet, no completed internal market (ibid., 435–47). There are, as ever, lots of promises of jam to come, but no jam today. Milward concludes:

> This is not surprising, when in the past to equip the European Communities with a parliament which replicated national democracy would have been needlessly to curb the states' powers to manage what was a restricted political device to provide additional support for policies already determined by national political parties. . . . The political machinery of the Union resembles the court of a minor eighteenth-century German state. There is a numerous and deferential attendance around the President of the

> Commission. A hierarchical bureaucracy attends to the myriad facets of relationships with the surrounding greater powers, for every decision has to be finely attuned to the wishes of the real powers to which the Union's continued existence is useful. (ibid., p. 446)

3 THE COMMUNITY AND THE NATION-STATE

We do not have to go far back in the history of the Community to find further evidence to support Milward's thesis. Examples abound, both historical and contemporary, particularly in those areas which have remained closest to the heart of the nation-state interest, such as economic policy. As Simon Bulmer has recently asserted, the Maastricht Treaty once again emphasises that economic integration has always been geared to the pervasive 'need to create a package deal satisfying the participants' national interests' (Bulmer, 1994, p. 5). Tsoukalis has made the same general observation, stressing the consistent failure to produce any genuine macroeconomic policies, both in times of economic recession and in periods of boom (Tsoukalis, 1991, chs. 2–3). During the 1970s, for example, the immediate response to the crises following the oil shock was to promote 'national champions' as a means of countering Community competition regulations. As François Duchenes has asserted, commenting on the effect of the 1970s recession: 'As usual, when great social and economic strains pull imperfectly cemented systems apart, there was a tendency to fall back on established loyalties and pyramids of authority, which were overwhelmingly national and, in broad economic times, bred protectionism' (Duchenes, 1990, pp. 15–19). According to Peter Montagnon, the continuing failure to establish a competition policy which can effect a free market is a testimony to the residual strength of the nation-states (Montagnon, 1990, pp. 100–4). Francis Snyder has reached a similar conclusion, emphasising the anomalous position in which the European Court has occasionally found itself, attempting to balance the rhetoric of the Commission with the clear reluctance of the nation-states actually to accede to it (Snyder, 1990, pp. 63–99).

Competition law, itself a loud admission of defeat in that 'pure' competition should not need the support of intricate legal regulation, in particular, is a mass of contradictions and inconsistencies resulting from the need to ameliorate particular national interests (Hornsby, 1987; Frazer, 1990). Competition policy is framed by considerable statute law and hedged by a fearsome array of statutory regulations. There are numerous obvious examples of such regulations being interpreted by the Court in order to accommodate the nation-states. Nationally sensitive industries, such as synthetic fibres and petrochemicals, continue to exist in a kind of twilight world apparently removed from the rigours of the new competitive Europe. One particular example is anti-dumping, the legislation for which remains practically useless, and is only intermittently enforced by a Commission which has anyway revealed itself to be far more interested in avoiding friction between internal and external Community trading partners (Kulms, 1990). Another is mergers. As Tsoukalis suggests, despite reforms which have appeared to redress the problem, the Merger Regulation threshold remains far too high really to effect any national mergers, and exists purely to support the member states against the threat of unwanted mega-mergers involving mulitnationals. The three most merger-active member states, the UK, France and Germany, have consistently opposed any reform of the merger thresholds (Tsoukalis, 1991, pp. 91–104). Similarly, state aids continue to grow across the Community, and will continue to do so, so long as the Council retains its right to validate exceptions to Article 92 (Gilchrist & Deacon, 1990, pp. 32–7). Perhaps the most striking and obvious example of the continuing presence of national interests as the motor of economic integration is the weakness of policies designed to effect greater regional equilibrium (Armstrong et al., 1994; George, 1991, pp. 295–309).

Although the rhetoric of the Commission has suggested that the great impediment to the single market is the retention of non-tariff barriers, many, and the most effective, still remain. As Damian Chalmers has recently emphasised, the European Court has studiously avoided immersing itself in the vexed questions of national price regulations. The recent *Keck* judgment, he adds, merely serves to emphasise this. Moreover, the whole attitude of the Court now, with regard to monitoring national economic policies, is more than ever one of 'consolidation rather than confrontation' (Chalmers, 1994, pp. 386–90, 401–3). Another famous example here, of course, is the *Woodpulp* decision, wherein the Court was prepared to accept national price-fixing arrangements if they could be justified as 'a rational response to the need to limit commercial risk in a long-term market' (*Woodpulp*; cf. Lange & Sandage, 1989). In other words, competition is fine, so long as it is not too competitive to the disadvantage of a particular national interest. As Tim Frazer has suggested, the future of competition law, as a kind of microcosm of Community economic law in general, remains uncertain. Commission rhetoric remains almost excessively optimistic; intensified competition will finally realise the hallowed ideal of the wholly free and unregulated market. There are, however, two alternative, less palatable and more likely probabilities. First, there is the very real possibility that the 'installation of the free market' will 'signify the triumph of free trade', but at the same time give rise to 'intensified anti-competitive recidivism' on the part of the would-be competitors. Second, and more pessimistically still, the member states will continue to promote the national interest over that of the Community, cling rigorously to currency sovereignty and intensify economic 'divergences' within the Community (Frazer, 1990, pp. 609–11). This danger has been recently acknowledged by the Director-General of DGIV, though he remains suitably confident that destiny will overcome it (Ehlermann, 1992, p. 259).

The nation-state economic interests remain in a state of good preservation, in most cases actually enhanced by European law. As McGee and Weatherill noted in 1990, there is no genuine free market, because it is not in the interests of the nation-states that there should be one: 'The political reality is that vested interests, both of national governments and of trade and professional organisations, seek to delay the creation of this kind of Common Market' (McGee & Weatherill, 1990, p. 578). This is precisely why there is still no single market, no single currency, and so on. The one measure which most commentators suggest could effect a genuinely free market and represent a corresponding economic and political diminution in national sovereignty, tax harmonisation, has remained strikingly absent from all the various reports, and is certainly conspicuous in its absence in the Maastricht Treaty (Pinder, 1993, pp. 53–9). To the extent that the common market has opened up during the 1980s and 1990s, it has only done so in so far as it has appeared to facilitate the national interests. The various Intergovernmental Conferences and summits which have heralded steps towards an internal market – Fontainebleau, Milan, Luxembourg, Edinburgh – have all been characterised by political compromises and the kind of backstairs jobbing which framed the Rome Treaty.

Neither is it difficult to find academic support for Milward's thesis. Writing in 1982, Stanley Hoffmann acknowledged that the 'most striking reality is not the frequent and well-noted impotence of the so-called sovereign state. It is its survival, despite the turmoil.' He concluded that 'the EEC regime is unique' in that it had 'served not only to preserve the nation-states, but paradoxically to regenerate them and to adapt them to the world of today' (Hoffmann, 1995, pp. 21, 35). Much more recently, Stephen George has suggested that the great failing in European integration studies is that of not presenting a theory of integration which takes note of the persistence of nationalism. It was this failure which ensured the ultimate demise of neo-functionalism, and nothing since has taken up the gauntlet (George, 1991, pp. 29–32, 226–30). Hans Kastendiek has suggested that any whimsical notion that the European Union will represent a shift of political power away from nation-states to some sort of transnational order is at best 'precipitate'. History tells us, he continues, that such 'convergences' hardly ever come about, unless by force, simply because the nation-states respond primarily to national pressures, and there can only be convergence if there is a coincidental 'emergence of similar problem constellations'. To date these have only been economic, and that will not be enough to effect a political response. Rather than 'convergence', Kastendiek suggests that the dominant theme in the Community is that of 'persistent diversity' (Kastendiek, 1990).

Although there is the 1992 Project, despite its rhetoric it remains almost exclusively an economic programme, and the actual political reality in Europe today is no more supranational in sympathy than it was in 1952. Lars Eriksson has noted the straightforward but none the less crucial equation between the controlled relinquishment of economic sovereignty, in return for a significantly enhanced political sovereignty on the part of the nation-states of Europe. Eriksson further suggests that the maintenance of political sovereignty in the nation-state is of paramount importance as a balance to the totalising, bureaucratic impulses of an economically determined single European 'state' (Eriksson, 1993). Jonathan Story has made a similar observation with regard to the Project which, even in its economic context, is no more than 'a state strategy . . . enacted in a multi-state Community whose member states are sovereign'. In more immediate terms, he suggests that the Project was a precise response to the particular problems experienced in France and Germany (Story, 1990, p. 47). The suggestion that the 1992 Project was always intended to be nothing more than a 'marketing exercise designed to create the impression that economic integration is an irreversible process' is a common one, as is the collateral suggestion that, given this rather limited, and indeed deceitful, ambition, there was never any remote question of actually effecting any complementary political or constitutional reform in the Maastricht Treaty (Campbell et al., 1990). Equally damning is Stephen George's dismissal of the resultant Delors 1992 Plan as something which 'bore all the hallmarks of a plan devised in Paris in the light of the failures of the 1981–4 French economic experiment'. If the Project and Delors Plan have any unifying purposes, they are to bolster the flagging French economy. The same precise national interests apply as they did when France initiated the ECSC and the Rome Treaty (George, 1991, p. 16).

Most recently, Milward, together with a number of other commentators, has developed this thesis by investigating further the historical and current ambitions of a number of member states. The preservation of the national interest, they conclude, is the common factor. The history of the Community and its individual member states reveals that,

> not only did virtually all power remain with the nation-state and its bureaucracy, with only limited surrenders of

> national sovereignty being made to integrationist institutions and only for narrowly defined purposes, but that states were also able to assert the priority of a national interest within the integrationist framework even against the wishes of large minorities of their populations or seemingly powerful interest groups. (Milward & Soerensen, 1993, p. 4)

It is this interest which continues to privilege interdependence over integration as the effective political reality in the new Union. This conclusion is reached in a number of complementary case-studies. Thus Federico Romero advances the thesis that Italy only joined the Community when it was assured of the privileged status of its migrant workers, and Frances Lynch reinforces the now more familiar argument that France joined the Community purely to maintain its agricultural base, whilst Vibeke Soerensen suggests that Denmark's consistently more ambivalent attitude to the Community, as recently illustrated in the attempt to ratify the Maastricht Treaty, is a corresponding result of the Community appearing to serve no obvious national interest (Romero, 1993, pp. 33–58; Lynch, 1993, pp. 59–87; Soerensen, 1993, pp. 88–116).

4 MAASTRICHT IN PERSPECTIVE

This is then the perspective from which we must assess the Maastricht Treaty. History emphasises that the extent to which the Community evolves is limited by the ambitions of the nation-states. The Community exists, not because it is a good idea, but because it can better serve these national interests. Although there was much rhetoric with regard to the desirability of a constitution which might better reflect the new Union, in reality there was not the same desirability on the part of the nation-states, and that is why such a constitution did not emerge. What emerged was more rhetoric, more aimless platitudes, and the textual and conceptual ambiguities which characterise political accommodation. Ultimately, the member states, as a corporate body, did not want Maastricht to realise any substantive constitutional reforms, and that, in turn, is why there were none. From a constitutional law perspective that might seem regrettable, but such is the nature of political reality. The Community is still very much a community of nation-states pursuing, as their primary concern, their respective national-interests. The text of the Maastricht Treaty is a testimony to this. Aside from its more immediate constitutional inadequacies, the strength of the nation-state interest can be further seen in the political shortcomings of the Treaty. Perhaps most obvious was a failure, yet again, to address the perceived 'democratic deficit'. The Council remains effectively unaccountable, and the Parliament effectively disempowered. As Philip Raworth has observed, the

> persistence of national particularism reflects a Community consciousness that is lacking or at least in its infancy. Thus, Parliament is yet an idiosyncratic body incorporating a European identity that is still artificial. . . . Such a body, directly elected or not, cannot yet dominate the legislative process.

At best, he concludes, politically, Maastricht is a very 'timid' step forward (Raworth, 1994, pp. 22–3). Martin Holland has similarly suggested that post-Maastricht Europe will remain firmly intergovernmental rather than supranational until it addresses the 'fundamental constitutional weakness' which the disempowerment of the Parliament represents (Holland, 1993, pp. 203–6). The existence of the Protocols is further evidence of the residual strength of the nation-state mentality in the new Union. The UK government perceives that the opt-out from the Social Charter is beneficial because it furnishes an advantage over other member states.

It is the nation-state, then, which remains to block European integration, and the rewriting of a more substantive and coherent European constitution. There is nothing God-given about nation-states. They are merely the residue of a particular European history. As Horsman and Marshall have suggested, the nation-state, the epitome of the modernist polity, is simply a 'way of imaging the world', in order to try to legitimate the exercise of power as the art of government (Horsman & Marshall, 1995, p. 269). But they have created a certain mystique around themselves, and it is this mystique which serves to nourish the nation-state. This is the political-cultural aspect of the nation-state. People react, almost reflexively, against threats to the nation-state. To use Dworkinian parlance, people have a positive 'attitude' towards nation-states. As Milward himself observes, the 'argument that the Europeanization of policy necessarily usurps national democratic control treats the abstract concept of sovereignty as though it were a real form of political machinery' (Milward, 1992, p. 446). Most people, across Europe, thus think of politics as national politics. Europe remains a distant abstraction, consciously ill-defined, because it is in the interests of the nation-states that it should be so. Attempts to ratify the Maastricht Treaty, particularly in France and Denmark, revealed just how successful the nation-states have been. There will be no further progress towards a European constitution unless it becomes clear that such a step is unavoidable to the interest of the nation-states (ibid., pp. 446–7). As Milward and Soerensen have concluded, the Maastricht Treaty is as much a treaty of intergovernmentalism as was the Rome Treaty. Although there is lip-service paid towards the idea of monetary union, there are no specific macro-integrational commitments. Aside from the constitutional shortcomings which we have already noted, there is a corresponding absence of any concrete political commitments to integration. The policy-making function remains squarely with the nation-states. The 'frontier of national sovereignty' in the new European Union is no more threatened than it was in 1952 or 1957. Indeed, it is stronger post-Maastricht than it ever was before (Milward & Soerensen, 1993, pp. 30–1).

4 The Limits of European Integration

The legal integration of Europe is limited, and it is limited for the same reasons as the European constitution is, as we have just seen, also limited. The very term 'integration' seems to imply progress towards some given end. And yet, in today's Europe there is no such given end. If there is progress, it is uncertain and not defined by any clear direction or impetus. There is no direction because there is no ultimate destination which the member states, in a corporate sense, are prepared to admit. The mythology of European integration is, at once, also the limitation of European integration. The experience of legal integration, like the experience of political integration, has been no more confused and confusing than in the UK. This chapter takes a particular look at this experience so that the extent of these limitations, or constitutional margins, can be more clearly defined.

The inadequacies of European legal integration in the UK can no longer be ascribed to newness or unfamiliarity. We have been in Europe long enough now, more than two decades, to have got things right, or near enough. But, quite plainly, we have not. The immediate purpose of this chapter is, then, to reveal the depth of this failure, and perhaps, to suggest some of the reasons. The first part will discuss the nature of British constitutional thought and its role in attempting to accommodate alternative theories of integration. The second part will illustrate these constitutional shortcomings in the light of various recent attempts on the part of the domestic judiciary to come to terms with the European challenge. Finally, I shall suggest the extent to which we, in the UK, will have to readjust ourselves, with a greater degree of integrity, to the demands which the politics of European integration require of the law.

1 THE FICTION OF DUALISM

The British constitution has always suffered from a particular flaw in its makeup. That flaw is the doctrine of parliamentary sovereignty. The idea of sovereignty itself is not necessarily problematic. Indeed it is difficult to envisage any legal order, except for the most primitive, which does not accommodate a notion of sovereignty somewhere. Steeped as we are in the UK in a particular Austinian and Hartian jurisprudential tradition, sovereignty lies at the heart of our constitutional thinking (Hart, 1961; cf. MacCormick, 1981; Bradley, 1994). It is the locus of sovereignty which is the problem, and it is a problem which has been bequeathed to us through the vagaries of our political history (Carty, 1991; cf. Munro, 1987, pp. 79–81). The execution of one king in 1649, and the deposition of another in 1688, effected a subtle, but critical, shifting of constitutional power, within a complex political and social elite. Hobbes's *Leviathan* was compromised by Locke's thesis of parliamentary sovereignty. According to Locke, God had vested civil sovereignty in Adam, and he had bequeathed it to the civil magistracy, the sovereign in Parliament. This is the 'nature' of the early modern social contract (Hobbes, 1985; Locke, 1989; cf. Carty, 1991, pp. 185–93; Kenyon, 1966; Lessnoff, 1986, ch. 4).

Whereas other nations, in both Europe and North America, were subsequently to experience popular revolution which, at least nominally, vested sovereignty in its people, its citizens, when the smoke cleared across the constitutional battlefield in late seventeenth-century Britain, sovereignty lay in Parliament, and not in the people. There is no Rousseau or Kant in our constitutional tradition, and thus no concept of popular sovereignty. Whereas, before 1649, the pervasive ambition had been to 'balance' the constitution, after 1688, it was to entrench the fiction of the 'monarch in Parliament' (Kenyon, 1966; Burgess, 1992). Constitutional power resides in the Parliament, and the people remain subject to it. Thus after three hundred years, the unavoidable anomaly exists, in the wake of the Maastricht Treaty, that we are now subjects of the Crown and citizens of Europe. We enjoy a twin political and legal identity.

It might be thought that such an archaic fiction which, as political historians acknowledge, was born of the desire of one social and religious elite to impress its authority over another, could now be comfortably abandoned, more a cause of belated relief than any particular sense of loss (Speck, 1988, chs. 7–10). This, however, is not the case. The reason for this, quite simply, is that socially, religiously, economically and politically, the UK has remained stagnant since the end of the seventeenth century. It is still ruled by the same male, white, Protestant, propertied middle classes, which emerged supreme from the great and so-called 'Glorious Revolution' of 1688 (Hill, 1986; Postema, 1986, ch. 7). Seen in this perspective, it is no longer surprising that the ancient constitution should still be today's constitution, and that parliamentary sovereignty should still be its fulcrum.

Although repeatedly rejected by political orders which the UK constitutional tradition is so-often alleged to have influenced, the doctrine of parliamentary sovereignty survives seemingly almost immune to criticism. In countless law school classrooms each autumn, constitutional law courses will open by emphasising the centrality of parliamentary sovereignty in our constitution. Sadly, on all too many occasions, it will be complemented by suggestions that parliamentary sovereignty is a good thing, because it somehow enshrines the fundamental principles of democracy. Yet, there is no trace of parliamentary sovereignty in the Platonic or Aristotelian tradition, from where the democratic tradition evolved. Indeed a conception of purely political, as opposed to ethical-political, sovereignty only arrives with the Socratic–Thomist synthesis, because Aquinas had a God to accommodate in the Aristotelian inheritance, and more importantly, the King of France (D'Entreves, 1987). Parliamentary sovereignty, as the textbooks evidence, emerges as a kind of transcendental given, beyond the realm of critical criticism. Antony Carty refers to its apparent 'alreadythereness', which seems to place it beyond criticism. A critique of parliamentary sovereignty is thus treated as little more than a damnable heresy (Carty, 1991, pp. 203–6). Yet, in reality, it is solely the product of historical chance and the particularities of medieval Europe and then seventeenth-century Britain. The real problem with parliamentary sovereignty is that we believe in it. Allan refers to its place in our 'political morality' (Allan, 1992, pp. 280–6). In fact, its strength lies in our constitutional psychology, not in any political or jurisprudential rationale. As Denis MacShane has suggested, it is this psychology which is then translated into a popular consciousness and then, in turn, consciously primitivised in popular political debate about the perceived 'threat' of Brussels (MacShane, 1995, pp. 23–35).

After three centuries of constitutional stagnation, the first real threat to the triumph of parliamentary sovereignty has come with our accession to the European Community. Once again, it is perhaps instructive to understand the historicity of our accession. Britain joined the Community, as we have already seen, not because it wanted to, but because it had to. Political power, in the modern world, is founded, ultimately, upon economic power. Since 1945 the UK has been economically untenable as an independent unit. Indeed, economically it had been in decline for over a century. The same rigid economic structures which had complemented and reinforced the social and political structures which had been established in the seventeenth and eighteenth centuries had singularly failed to move 'beyond' the 'modern' into the 'post' modern. Economically, we now inhabit a pluralist and participatory world, where economic power cannot be so readily identified and, most importantly, determined in any particular situation.

As a number of commentators have noted, in economic terms, the world has moved past the nation-state, on the one hand, consolidating power in multinationals, thus complementing the so-called 'global' economy, whilst, on the other hand, devolving power down past the nation-state into the hands of microeconomic units. By way of an example, as Stuart Holland has recently emphasised, the debate over national currency sovereignty is another of the fictions in current integration debate. The large, multinational economic enterprises have controlled so-called 'national' currencies since the end of the 1970s, if not before. In economic reality there is no such thing as a national currency (Holland, 1993, pp. 31–5). As Martin Heidegger noted, the *technē* of a post-modern economics will be realised in the monster devouring its creator, the 'modern' state (Heidegger, 1977, pp. 3–35). There is, of course, a fundamental irony here. As Milward suggests, the UK joined the Community precisely to preserve itself as a nation-state. The UK joined the Community because it was the best, indeed the only, way of maintaining the integrity of the nation-state. The UK's survival, paradoxically, appeared to depend upon the strength of the European Community. For the British political establishment, and its constitutional fiction, the trick lay in maximising the economic benefit of accession, whilst minimising its constitutional concessions. How could parliamentary sovereignty be preserved as the keystone of the British constitutional structure, whilst accommodating the reality of a rival political and legal order which, through its courts, had increasingly claimed judicial sovereignty? European Community law, as the European Court had very rapidly emphasised, is supreme over any domestic law (*Costa*; *Simmenthal*; cf. Wyatt & Dashwood, 1993, pp. 56–8). Thus European politics, by necessary implication, is supreme over national politics. The real 'threat' of European law is the supremacy of European politics and European political theory.

Much is made in contemporary debate about the perceived 'democratic deficit' in the new Europe. As we shall see in the next chapter, this particular debate is one of the great distractions in contemporary European political dialogue, assuming, as it does, a particular definition of democracy and the corresponding exclusion of the real debate about alternative democracy. It plays, in the UK, upon the particular psychology that democracy is realised if representatives are elected to a body which is then sovereign over all of us. The idea that political power might be radically dispersed amongst political structures, and balanced between them, is consciously marginalised. This is not to suggest that the European Union, as it stands, is a paragon of democratic virtue. It certainly is not. But, in its post-Maastricht condition, there is a potential for the dispersion of power. Neither the Union nor the UK enjoys a participatory or genuinely plural politics; but, as we shall see in the final chapter, at least the Union's 'constitution' enjoys the potential.

As we have seen, there is a European 'constitution' of sorts, traditionally founded upon the Treaty framework and supplemented by various collateral legislative and juridical forms. The development of this constitution, although itself much criticised for its inadequacies and incohesiveness, should not be underestimated. Although, as we have seen in the previous chapter, there is much contemporary dismay amongst legal commentators as to its perceived failings, the renewed impulse towards a more refined constitutional order, together with the ideological triumph of supranationalism over its intergovernmentalist rivals, suggests a renewed determination to realise the full democratic potential of the new European Union.

Nowhere is the potential of the new Union better evidenced than in the much maligned concept of subsidiarity, and, as we have already seen, various legal commentators have expended much energy upon the imprecision of a juridical definition of subsidiarity. But subsidiarity is not supposed to enjoy any particular legal definition. As a political concept which only enjoys a meaning in a particular political situation, it is consciously designed to evade singular definition (Peterson, 1994; Teasdale, 1993). As I shall suggest throughout this book, and particularly in the final chapter, subsidiarity, determinable only in the particular, can be presented as a classically post-modern conception. The perception of subsidiarity is that power should be exercised by those most affected by it, and not by those who assume responsibility for defining it and thus enforcing it. It is thus a participatory political concept, the resolution of which is realised in the particular. Its potential lies beyond the mere apportioning of power between 'European' and domestic 'national' political structures. Subsidiarity can represent, indeed define, a radically alternative understanding of democracy. Thus, as a threat to parliamentary sovereignty its potential is enormous, far greater than that ever anticipated in 1972. Post-Maastricht presents the possibility, not merely of sovereignty removed to Brussels, but of sovereignty returned to the new European citizen, and for this it must be cherished.

One thing is certain. The European 'constitution' has moved beyond that which could be 'dexterously' accommodated in 1972. Upon accession, faced with the challenge of Europe and European law, the UK Parliament arrogated for itself a fictional sovereignty over Europe by drafting and approving the 1972 European Communities Act, and then left the jurisprudential accommodation to its judges. It was not to be disappointed. There was never any question of the judiciary, in 1972, suggesting that parliamentary sovereignty might be in any way compromised. Despite Lord Denning's rather uncomfortable acknowledgement that European law was fundamentally alien to a British judge and required a radically different judicial attitude, in his preliminary encounter in *Bulmer*, subsequently, in *Macarthy's*, Denning obligingly effected his so-called 'dexterous revolution', according to which European law only enjoyed effect in the UK by the will of Parliament. European law was thus incorporated by the 1972 Act and limited by it. Parliamentary sovereignty was thus preserved. The possibility of express repeal of the 1972 Act remained to reinforce its authority. The fact that, economically and politically, withdrawal has been impossible has become increasingly obvious. To the more perceptive it was obvious in 1972. But parliamentary sovereignty demanded that there should be an illusion to which we could cling. Constitutional theory maintained a studious indifference to political reality, and the result, once again, is fiction. As Ian Harden has recently emphasised, the continuing dislocation between political and legal conceptions of sovereignty lies at the heart of our present constitutional accommodation and its inadequacies (Harden, 1994, pp. 612–13).

What Lord Denning further emphasised in the two cases was that European law, subject to parliamentary sovereignty, thus exists as a component, or sub-species, of our legal order. European law, in our dual constitution, is separate from domestic law. The existence of a dualist constitution, of course, necessarily militates against the very idea of integration. It is designed to prevent integration. Indeed, the entire jurisprudential psyche seems to be geared against integration, and as much so now as it was in 1972 (ibid., p. 611). Law schools run courses in 'European law', quite separate from domestic law. Such courses should not be necessary, still less exist. They presume that students can study contract law in isolation from European contract law, commercial law in isolation from European commercial law, and so on. The recent 'elevation' of European law as a putatively compulsory' course approved by the Law Society is a condemnation of our jurisprudential approach to Europe, not a vindication of it. It further impresses upon the psychology of lawyers, teachers and students that European law is a 'separate' option, no more inherently a part of 'UK' legal studies than options in comparative US law, or for that matter nineteenth-century Russian literature or polymer chemistry. UK law, in UK law schools, remains the norm, and European legal studies remain outside the norm. Indeed, it is now officially 'required' that UK law students should have to study European law as a separate entity. The impact of this approach can be similarly evidenced in student texts. Take, for example, administrative law. The traditional authority, Wade and Forsyth's *Administrative Law*, accomplishes the quite extraordinary feat of almost exclusively marginalising European Community administrative law. Out of over one thousand pages, European Community administrative law is referred to in passing on no more than two dozen occasions. The fact that its chief rival, Craig's *Administrative Law*, devotes entire chapters to the European dimension only serves to exacerbate the apparent inconsistencies.

In our Foucauldian world of 'specialized knowledges', the universities have emerged as the bastions of the political elite (Derrida, 1983). By separating and defining the limits of knowledge, universities define knowledge itself. The same, of course, is true of university teachers and university textbooks. As Jacques Derrida has recently affirmed, this universal trend is no more immediately apparent than in the study and exposition of European politics and law (Derrida, 1992, pp. l–lii). Just as law is so often studied in isolation from its political, social and economic contexts, so too is European law studied in a particular dual isolation, from its political, social and economic context, and from 'us', from our law and our domestic law. The sense of remoteness is all the greater. The law relating to Europe is separate somehow from the law relating to us in the UK.

2 THE CONSEQUENCES OF THE FICTION

Fictions, by definition, are designed to hide the truth. They are written with specific audiences in mind, with the ambition of arresting that audience and satiating it. The British, as loyal subjects of their Queen in Parliament, were to be satiated, and comforted, by Lord Denning's fiction. Parliament was common sovereign over a dual constitution comprising both domestic law and European law. Fictions should not, however, be allowed to impact upon reality. With the benefit of hindsight, it can be appreciated that Denning's fiction was as much intended to provide a psychological release as a practical juridical one. Unfortunately, his 'revolution' has effected a considerable and wholly undesirable impact upon the reality of law in the UK. The extent of the impact, and its undesirability, can be evidenced in a whole series of pronouncements in the area of administrative law.

Administrative law is peculiar in that it has been in the vanguard of legal harmonisation in the new Europe, but unlike such as contract law, not through EC legislation, but rather through the activism of the European Court of Justice. The importance of this activism has been noted by a number of commentators, including former judges, Koopmans, Mackenzie Stuart and Slynn (Koopmans, 1991; Mackenzie Stuart, 1987; Slynn, 1987). Most recently, Jürgen Schwarze, in a substantial and essentially comparative analysis of European Court and member state court decisions, has pointed to a 'convergence' thesis, which suggests that the European Court, through a series of judgments including such as *Transocean Marine Paint, National Panasonic* and *Heylens,* has sought to effect harmonisation, not just between the European Court and the member states, but also between member state courts throughout the Community (Schwarze, 1992). At the same time, in complementary fashion, the European Court has consistently supported the employment of certain principles of administrative law, such as legitimate expectations and proportionality. Similarly, by developing its direct effect jurisprudence, the Court has required the regularisation of remedial effectiveness. Cases such as *Factortame* and *Francovich* have necessitated the extension of remedies, which in certain jurisdictions including the UK were only available in private law, to public law. In order fully to effect EC law directives, and thus implicitly the supremacy of EC law, member state courts are now required to support injunctions against public law bodies, which, if need be, effect temporary or permanent disapplication of domestic law, as in *Factortame*, and also damages against public law bodies, as in *Francovich* (*Factortame*; *Francovich*; cf. de Burca, 1992; cf. Steiner, 1993; Craig, 1993).

Unsurprisingly, the UK judiciary has reacted with some distaste to their implicit powers of constitutional review. Thus, in *Factortame*, Lord Bridge clung tenaciously to the myth that in granting an injunction against government legislation, he was in fact acting in support of parliamentary sovereignty, rather than in review of it (*Factortame*, pp. 1021–2). Implicit in his ruling is the assumption that full and effective remedies against public law bodies exist solely in actions which allege some breach of European law, as opposed to domestic law. This suspicion is further enhanced by comments made in both the Court of Appeal and the House of Lords, in *M v Home Office* and *In re. M* (*M v Home Office*; *In re. M*; cf. Ward, 1994b). In both cases individual judges expressed themselves to be uncomfortable with the dichotomy which now currently exists between remedies in European public law and those in domestic public law. According to Lord Donaldson, in the Court of Appeal, such a dichotomy is 'anomalous, and . . . wrong in principle'. In the House of Lords, Lord Woolf confessed himself to being 'unhappy' at the inevitable inconsistency and incoherence. What is most revealing, however, is that, although it was clear that the judges acknowledged the greater potential justice effected by remedies available in European public law, because *M* did not involve any definable European law issue, they refused to take advantage of a more radical, and just, alternative. The dual constitution not only allowed certain judges to avoid acknowledging the possibility of injunctions against Crown ministers, it encouraged this avoidance (Ward, 1994c).

One of the more astonishing lacunae in UK administrative law is the fact that administrative law bodies are not required to give the reasons for their decisions. In *ex p Cunningham*, though clearly troubled by the anomaly, Lord Donaldson suggested that the case for a right to reasons was 'unarguable' (*Cunningham*). This was despite the fact that the European Court had recently ruled, in the *Heylens* case, that a right to reasons is a fundamental administrative right, founded as a fundamental right (*Heylens*). As Schwarze has emphasised, in *Heylens* the European Court was making explicit the desire that such fundamental rights should be universally applied regardless of any pretended dichotomy between European and domestic law. According to Schwarze, *Heylens* represents the apogee of the 'convergence' thesis (Schwarze, 1991, p. 14). Despite this, in *Cunningham* the Court of Appeal did not even pay passing witness to the European Court. *Cunningham* was not a European law case, and so, once again, the doctrine of the dual constitution forbade application of principles introduced in European public law no matter how patently appropriate they might appear to be. More recently, in *Doody* and in *Walters*, whilst appearing to soften the judicial stance, and in *Walters* actually acknowledging that a right to reasons might exist in UK domestic law, once again there was conspicuously no attempt to justify the introduction of the principle by citing the judicial policy of the European Court (*Doody*; *Walters*; cf. Campbell, 1994). The European Court may talk of fundamental administrative law rights to be enjoyed by the citizens of Europe, but UK courts still hold dear to the notion of discretionary administrative law remedies which may or may not be enjoyed by the Queen's subjects.

Perhaps the most striking example of judicial obstructiveness with regard to a principle of potential constitutional import has been the intermittent application of proportionality in domestic courts. It is quite clear, as Schwarze emphasises, that the European Court intends proportionality to be a harmonising concept, of application across the Union. This was emphasised by the Court in its response to the first reference in the Sunday trading litigation, from the Cwmbran magistrates (*Torfaen*). In the opinion of the European Court, the sensible and consistent application of proportionality was the most effective way of resolving the numerous Sunday trading cases which lay before UK courts. What actually ensued, however, was jurisprudential chaos. As Richard Rawlings has observed, the domestic courts were given a concept which, both jurisprudentially and psychologically, they were not 'remotely equipped to handle' (Rawlings, 1993, p. 317). Various courts reached different conclusions, not least because some decided to employ proportionality, whilst some chose to ignore it. Amongst those who chose to employ it, some thought that it did require the abrogation of the Shops Act, whilst others thought not. Hoffman J., in *Stoke on Trent*, decided that the virtues of the 'traditional English Sunday' outweighed constitutional nicety. While in the *Peterborough* case, Lord Mustill expressed himself to be uncertain as to whether keeping 'the Sabbath Holy' was more fundamental than the constitutional jurisprudence of the 'Common market' (Rawlings, 1993).

Perhaps the most remarkable proportionality ruling in UK domestic courts is *ex p Brind* (*Brind*). Here, only months after handing down his judgment in *Factortame*, Lord Bridge impressed once again the dichotomy in the UK constitution. The powers of constitutional review, which are clearly intended by the European Court, are to be marginalised to purely European law matters. Lord Roskill conceded that the situation might change in time, but was reluctant as yet to recognise proportionality as a fundamental constitutional principle. Lord Ackner, in rhetoric which decried what he perceived to be the incipient imperialism of the European Court, openly refused to apply a principle which he readily admitted that he did not fully understand. Ignorance of the law is supposed to be no defence. But it seems to be okay for the judges. In the *Peterborough* case, Lord Mustill used it as his justification for electing not to use proportionality (*Peterborough*). It is the fact that the court in *Brind* emphasised that the case did not involve any distinct European law matter which makes it all the more noteworthy. Lord Ackner went out of his way, not only to maintain the fiction of a dual constitution, but also to condemn the appropriateness of proportionality in domestic law. Merely ignoring it was not enough. Ackner clearly did not share any sense of discomfort or 'unhappiness' at the apparent inconsistencies which lie between European and domestic administrative law. Indeed, he relished the discrepancies. In some judicial circles at least, Lord Denning's 'dexterous revolution' is still very much alive and kicking. Although one or two judges might voice their disquiet, for the vast majority,

European and UK law remain rigidly distinct, and rights in European law remain quite distinct from those in domestic law. Jurisprudential dissatisfaction at the resulting inconsistencies remains subservient to the overriding need to satisfy the psychology of parliamentary sovereignty.

3 BEYOND DUALISM

It is quite obvious that European law is not yet fully harmonised, neither in the UK nor indeed anywhere else. There are, as Schwarze suggests, undeniable 'tendencies' towards 'convergence'. But there are equally obvious limits. It might reasonably be suggested that in the UK we are perhaps further away than many of our fellow member states. Moreover, on a wider scale, it might be similarly suggested that European–UK integration is also a long way short of realisation. As long as the myth of constitutional dualism remains, there will be little further progress towards legal integration. Dualism precludes integration, by definition. In a recent and compelling essay, Neil MacCormick has suggested that, in terms of constitutional jurisprudence, we must rid ourselves of the shackles of unitary parliamentary sovereignty (MacCormick, 1993). Wade has made the same implication (Wade, 1991). So too has Paul Craig, in a telling critique of Lord Bridge's attempt to resuscitate the dualist fiction in *Factortame* (Craig, 1991, pp. 252–5). More precisely, what this requires is a movement beyond an archaic, and now fictional, understanding of our constitution, towards one which is appropriate for the next millenium. Such a constitutional understanding can only be realised in an alternative radical, participatory democratic polity. One, in other words, which is post-Dicey and post-modern (cf. Harden, 1994, pp. 612–13).

As Trevor Smith has recently suggested, the British constitution is now 'unravelled'. A post-modern critique, he adds, 'reveals a political system disorientated, deficient and out of sorts with itself'. The post-modern ambition, he suggests, is to 're-mobilise consent in order to legitimise a new set of constitutional arrangements'. The remobilisation can only come about, he concludes, by the fragmenting of sovereignty to the previously dislocated citizen (Smith, 1994). As we shall see in the final chapter, this is a view which is increasingly widely supported. According to Simon Hix (1994), this fragmentation of sovereignty is common across Europe. A new European constitutional order, he suggests, will be quite unlike anything which has supported the nation-state for the last two centuries. Ruggie makes a similar observation. The post-modern politics of Europe, he insists, requires us to 'unbundle' the discourse of modernist politics (Ruggie, 1993).

Thus, a post-modern constitution, to the extent that one can be 'defined', will be one in which sovereignty is fragmented. This is not a 'pooling' of sovereignty, as is so often suggested. A 'pooling' of sovereignty merely shares sovereignty amongst a group of nation-states. A post-modern devolution of sovereignty removes it from the exclusive possession of one, or all, of the nation-states. Sovereign power is fragmented, both across the Union and from community to community, and individual to individual. This, of course, is one, admittedly the more radical, definition of subsidiarity. Ian Harden has suggested that subsidiarity is a 'recognition' of a need, rather than a 'specific principle'. It encapsulates a spirit of participatory democracy. In this context, he suggests that subsidiarity 'is not just about the relationship between States and the Union, but also about the search for a richer variety of collectivities, political and otherwise, which individuals can use as a meaningful context for their actions'. In this way a post-Diceyan and post-modern constitutionalism can envisage a Union without a state. There can be a representation of community and solidarity, without a unified state sovereignty, determined by 'institutions with different, separate, forms of accountability, appropriate to their specific tasks' (Harden, 1994, pp. 613, 629, 624).

The Maastricht Treaty, as I have already suggested, has attracted much criticism. To a certain extent this is deserved. There is much obfuscation, little clarity. But the magnitude of the political revolution which it potentialises in the UK, as elsewhere across the new Europe, should not be underestimated. Participatory democracy cannot be born in one Treaty, and political reality in much of Europe today militates against a more overt revolution. It should, however, be remembered just how close the politicians came at

Maastricht to actualising something more concrete. Only the vestigial forces of UK parliamentary sovereignty and its psychological impact upon certain sections of the British Conservative Party defeated the inclusion of an overtly federal ambition in the final draft of the Treaty. Ultimately, the Maastricht Treaty was indeed a series of compromises and accommodations. Such is in the very nature, perhaps, of modern transnational agreements. Each and every member state of the new Union is a reflexive nation-state first, and a component of the Union second. The continuing strength of the nation-state should not be underestimated. But neither should it be thought to be insurmountable. At present, its fate is very much in the balance. The height of these political stakes explains just why there is so much contemporary rhetoric in the UK with regard to the threat to parliamentary sovereignty. If it falls, then so does so much of the psychology of the sovereign nation-state. As Andrew Moravcsik reminds us, the struggle between the rival ideologies of supranationalism and intergovernmentalism is a bitter and enduring one. It is his conclusion that the politics of Europe will always be a compromise. Correspondingly, then, political integration will always be limited by political reality and by the vested interest of the nation-state (Moravcsik, 1994).

Legal integration, however, can lead us to a rather different conclusion. Integration through law is not necessarily so limited. Legal integration is ultimately effected by lawyers, judges and courts, and not by politicians. Likewise the limitations and failings so apparent in our present jurisprudential condition are the responsibility of our lawyers and judges, not our politicians. As the European Court has increasingly urged, the real power lies with the lawyers. As the Critical Legal Studies movement has so often suggested, ultimately, real power in modern society always lies with lawyers (Kennedy, 1982). The limitations of legal integration are those established in the minds of lawyers. Ultimately, the reaction of the national judiciaries will determine the nature, and extent, of integration. We can, on the one hand, cling to fiction. That is the recommendation of some prominent leading academic commentators. Allan has recently suggested that in constitutional terms, our accession to the Community can be 'safely viewed as of little practical importance' (Allan, 1992, p. 274). Regardless of the veracity of this statement, it can also be suggested that this does not have to be the case. Practice can change. Other commentators suggest that parliamentary sovereignty no longer exists (cf. Anav, 1989). Unfortunately, it does exist. It exists so long as lawyers and judges want to pretend that it does. The day we liberate ourselves from the oppressive psychology of unitary parliamentary sovereignty, and the fiction of dualism, is the day we embrace the spirit of European integration. The spirit of the new Europe, its politics and its jurisprudence, demand that member state courts join the European Court in better effecting a coherent and uniform European constitution, one founded upon a concept of fundamental right, not mere discretion, and under which all bodies, public and private, are subject to a rule of law, which is itself founded upon by the radical decentralisation and fragmentation of sovereignty. Integrity must replace incoherence, and reality fiction. But it can only do so in a world which is properly understood by nation-states to be beyond the nation-state.

5 (Pre)conceptions in European Law

The new European Union is trying hard; or so it seems. It is trying to be more democratic, to be closer to us, the new European citizens, to give us rights, to make us all better off. It is trying to set an agenda. Of course, the Community has always had an agenda. The Community was designed to reinforce peace in Europe, and to make money. More particularly, it was designed to preserve the authority of the nation-state and its prosperity. Wealthy and secure citizens of the post-war nation-states, it was surmised, would make happy and contented citizens. As I suggested in chapter 3, the history of the Community has always been a history of preserving the nation-state interest, and of making the minimum necessary concessions to the much vaunted supranational characteristics established in the Treaty framework. The situation has changed during the last decade; or at least it has appeared to change. The apparent catalyst for the change has been the determination to complete the single market, encapsulated in the '1992 Project'. The increasing realisation of the Commission, that economic integration necessitated greater political integration, has given the Community and Union an ambition which for the previous three decades had remained purely rhetorical.

In this chapter, I want to subvert certain of the fundamental premises which have lain behind the determination to effect greater political integration, and I want to do so by addressing certain key concepts which, I shall suggest, have been presumed in the present discourse surrounding the new political Union. There has been much talk about making the Union more democratic. The talk has presumed a certain vision of democracy. Similarly, there has been much talk about the virtues of European citizenship. Once again, a particular idea of citizenship is presumed. These are the two preconceptions upon which I want to concentrate. They are not, however, the only such preconceptions, and, as the chapter progresses, I shall suggest that concepts such as sovereignty and rights are similarly preconceived. The reason for the preconceptions is not difficult to surmise. They are the same preconceptions which lie at the heart of the visions of democracy and citizenship which substantiate and justify the primacy of the nation-state in our traditional political discourse. Ultimately, I shall suggest in the final section of this chapter, what we are really talking about here are issues of definition and identity. What are the preconceptions with which the new Europe is being described, and what are the possible altenatives?

1 DEMOCRACY

From those who perceive the apogee of democracy to be the intermittent ability to vote for certain pre-selected candidates, there has been much talk of the 'democratic deficit'. Perhaps unsurprisingly, the loudest talk has been from those who have confirmed the sanctity of representative democracy, by participating most actively in it. Shirley Williams has thus decried the 'gap' between those powers transferred to Brussels from Westminster, and 'our' ability to control these powers. If those we elect as MEPs had the same powers of supervision as those we elect as MPs, the logic goes, then all would be well. Writing in 1990–1 she suggested that the movement towards greater 'joint-decisionmaking', most immediately between the Commission and the Parliament, represented an important step forward. Williams talked about the need for 'anger' and 'passion' in European politics, and even the need to enhance the 'participation' of the European citizen, but that participation went as far as the ballot-box and no further (S. Williams, 1991).

The role of the European Parliament in this 'joint-decisionmaking' process, as refined in the Single European Act, was fractionally enhanced by the Maastricht Treaty on European Union. The Treaty introduced the so-called co-decision procedure, in Article 189B, by which Parliament maintains its influence in the second, as well as the first, round of inter-institutional legislative negotiations. It thus enjoys, at least in theory, an absolute right to reject legislation.

However, as a number of critics have noted, this procedure still does not give Parliament the final say with regard to the legislative process. All legislation must still be approved by the Council. The new Union thus remains, we are informed, fundamentally undemocratic (Raworth, 1994). I would not dispute this conclusion. But in what sense is it undemocratic? What I want to dispute, once again, is the implied premise that if Parliament did have the final say on legislative matters, then the European Union would be a thoroughly democratic polity. This same implication can be found in so many similar post-Maastricht critiques (Nicholl, 1994; Corbett, 1994; Pinder, 1994). The preconception is widely shared. A democratic Europe is defined as a representatively democratic Europe.

It does not have to be so. Indeed, if the new Europe offers one particular possibility with regard to theories of governance, it is that of radical, alternative theories of democracy. In part it does so because, to some extent or other, the new Europe has compromised the nation-state and presented a political and constitutional theory which, as Neil McCormick has suggested, is 'beyond the sovereign state' (MacCormick, 1993). As we saw in the previous chapter, the assumption, which has lain at the heart of English constitutional jurisprudence in particular, that sovereignty must lie in one body, personal or corporate, has already been subverted. Indeed, it is the mainspring of many federalist models for the new Europe. Ernest Wistrich has recently re-emphasised that federalism requires a dispersion of sovereignty. However, although a federal model may disperse sovereignty, it does not necessarily disperse power or encourage an alternative vision of democracy. A federal state is no less a state than a nation-state, and its democratic lifeblood is similarly representative. Wistrich, indeed, is anxious to reassure us that a federal Europe can be as representatively democratic as any nation-state. The new Europe, he suggests, must impress upon us its thoroughly democratic nature by redefining itself precisely as a federal 'state'. Interestingly, Wistrich admits that if the European Union does not reform its political processes in such a way, the very idea of representative democracy in Europe runs the risk of becoming 'discredited'. This, he continues, would be a bad thing (Wistrich, 1994, pp. 97–114). But would it?

If political power is no longer concentrated in any one body, then there is far less need for complementary theories of democracy to favour the representative model. Everyone can play an active part in democracy. In other words, and to use contemporary critical parlance, everyone can 'participate' directly, as opposed to representatively, in democratic governance. The natural complement to participatory democracy is pluralism. The dispersion of power enhances the real possibility of participation in government. Indeed, it creates a duty or obligation of self-government. The possibilities of a plural and participatory democratic model for post-Maastricht Europe have been tentatively explored by David Coombes. In sharp contrast to such as Wistrich, Coombes suggests that the European Union neither is, nor should aim to be, federal in the established sense of a federal state. The alternative is a kind of 'sub-species of confederation', which is itself part of a wider movement in international relations to find alternatives to traditional theories of state sovereignty. Pluralism, he rightly suggests, is characterised as a reaction against both the nation-state and the European state, against both nationalism and supranationalism. Perceptively, he continues by suggesting that pluralism can be distinguished as a form of 'social' as opposed to political integration. At the same time, and this will become more important in the second section of this chapter, as a socially determined idea of governance, pluralism will be supplemented by a social, as opposed to political, determination of citizenship and rights. Coombes concludes his critique of Union governance by appealing for a more radical agenda:

> If Europeans could successfully develop an alternative approach to the government of political communities and the relations between them, they would not only be responding to their own needs but also providing the kind of influence, by example, that is the only truly effective way of both defending one's own enjoyment of pluralist values pertaining to a civil society and ensuring their ultimate availability to others. (Coombes, 1994, pp. 177–8)

If we really want to access such a radical alternative vision of democracy, I would suggest that we shall need to explore the full potential of both participation and pluralism outside either the nation-state or federal-state models. Such an alternative has already been suggested by Jürgen Habermas as being perhaps appropriate in the context of the new European Union (Habermas, 1992, p. 2). Neither participatory democracy nor pluralism is a new idea. During the 1980s the Critical Legal Studies movement consistently placed much weight upon the idea of enhancing citizen participation in government, at the same time as advancing pluralism as the natural complement to participatory democracy. Seminal essays, such as Peter Gabel's 'The Phenomenology of Rights-Consciousness', revolved around the ambition of 'transforming public space' and effecting 'participatory politics' (Gabel, 1984, p. 1596). The pluralist model was most immediately espoused in ideas of enhanced local politics, or what James Boyle termed 'local social thought' (Boyle, 1985). Such forms of regional pluralism were popular. Jerry Frug urged the establishment of participatory democracy in communities as 'administrative democracy', effected by the radical decentralisation of power to 'units small enough to make popular participation in government decision-making feasible' (Frug, 1990, p. 574). Alternative models sought to marry participatory democracy and pluralism in the workplace. Karl Klare suggested that industrial democracy had to be more than merely enhancing the representative status of group interests. In other words, industrial power had to be exercised by workers making decisions, not merely delegating responsibility to representatives. Rather, it was tied to reforming the very nature of modern societal relations, and demanded the establishment of 'entirely new ways of organizing social life, new conceptions of social relationships and of community, work and democratic governance' (Klare, 1982a, p. 200). Participatory democracy in practice would facilitate the 'effort to conceptualize work as an experience of free, creative expression and the workplace as a locus of democratic self-governance' (Klare, 1982b, p. 84).

As an alternative, some of the most interesting and immediately appropriate writings on pluralism are of considerably older vintage. Like the CLS movement, the English pluralists, writing in the first part of this century, were driven by a desire to present a radical alternative to established theories of law and government. But whereas the CLS variants have tended to concentrate primarily, though not exclusively, on regional pluralism, and moreover have tended to critique the role of group interests in favour of enhancing the situation of the 'alienated' individual, the English pluralists stridently advocated the empowerment of functional interests in group form. The English pluralists, headed by such figures as Harold Laski, G.D.H. Cole and F.W. Maitland, shared the same broadly critical jurisprudential stance as the CLS movement. Above all, they adopted a philosophical scepticism towards any pretence of legal or political formalism. The three characteristics of their writings were, first, that liberty of the individual was the paramount political ideal; second, that such freedom could only be served by dispersing political sovereignty; and third, that these ambitions were best served by interest groups, enjoying real legal personality. The concentration of power in Westminster was a constant threat to the liberty of the individual, not a guarantor of it (Nicholls, 1994, pp. 4–16). These central tenets, as Paul Hirst has recently emphasised, serve to make English pluralism the most appropriate of models for the new Europe (Hirst, 1993, p. 8).

David Nicholls has suggested that this uncompromising critique of centralised sovereignty provided much of the intellectual fuel for the federal movements, which were beginning to emerge in English economic and political thought at the time, and which, in turn, were to be a major influence on the writings of such as Monnet and Spinelli. Moreover, the *Factortame* decision, he suggests, represents the realisation of Maitland's dream (Nicholls, 1994, pp. 33–4, 49–52). According to the English pluralists, the nation-state could only be defined as the constitution of sub-communities, and sovereignty must lie in that constitution of sub-communities. According to Laski, the state, as such, is simply one group amongst many, with the responsibility of regulating the politics which is created by the various interest groups which define the sub-communities (ibid., pp. 77–89). It is interesting that the English pluralists, again like the CLS movement, should situate a more immediately practical focus for their alternative theories of democracy in the workplace. The primary interest groups were economically and functionally determined. Most obviously, both Laski and Cole were interested in describing a political theory which could enhance the role of the trade unions and guilds as archetypal interest groups. The 'politics of industry', Laski prophesied, could supersede the politics of Westminster. Although such forms of pluralism would still be representative, because of their interest group constitution, the possibility of participation would be greatly enhanced. In such a politics, both employers and employees would share fully in the decision-making process (Hirst, 1993, pp. 36–8).

This situation for pluralist democracy, in the workplace, enjoys an obvious resonance in European studies, and European law, because the European Community has always been geared to the overarching determination to make money. It is, first and foremost, an economic enterprise, the success or otherwise of which rests squarely in the workplace. Famously, there was little in the Treaty of Rome to suggest a great deal of concern with social policy. Although there were occasional initiatives during the first few decades, most obviously the 1974 Social Action Programme, Stuart Holland, writing in 1980, voiced the concern of many in suggesting that the Community had 'abandoned' its citizens (Holland, 1980). Since the resurrection of the so-called 'new Social Action Programme', in 1984, there has been an increasing interest in the idea of 'social Europe', as a natural complement to the single market (Wise & Gibb, 1993, pp. 146–7). The centrepiece of 'social Europe' can be found in the workplace. A happier worker, it is surmised, will make for a more productive worker. The Commission was sufficiently convinced by the various reports of the Marin and Papandreou Committees, that it pressed for the acceptance of a Community Charter for the Social Rights of Workers in December 1989, which was accepted by everyone except the UK. The Charter made much of the need for the democratisation of the workplace and the virtue of greater worker participation in the form of 'collective bargaining' procedures. According to Commission President Jacques Delors, it represented the 'solemn declaration' of such an ambition. Unfortunately, it enjoyed no legal backing whatsoever (ibid., pp. 152–60). The idea of democratising the workplace returned in the Maastricht Treaty, where the Protocol on Social Policy noted that the eleven signatories of the 1989 Charter wished to 'continue along the path laid down', whilst the annexed Agreement on Social Policy established an ultimate goal of 'economic and social cohesion'. However, as we have already noted in chapter 2, the Protocol and Agreement remain wholly overshadowed by the pervasive economic ideology of the Treaty (cf. Shaw, 1994).

The Treaty does, however, introduce a tantalising and potentially more fruitful alternative, and that is subsidiarity. The rhetoric of Maastricht, at least in a constitutional sense, was dominated by the idea of subsidiarity. Subsidiarity might be a participatory and pluralist concept. Contemporary advocates of pluralism, such as Johannes Messner suggest that subsidiarity, understood in its established federal sense, is 'a fundamental principle of the pluralistic society' (Nicholls, 1994, p. 130). But there again it might not be. Subsidiarity can both justify the idea of state governance and provide a means to go beyond it (Coombes, 1994, p. 167). Jacques Delors, the President of the Commission at the time of the Treaty, certainly associated subsidiarity with pluralism. It should, he suggested, ensure the 'decentralised organisation of responsibilities, with the aim of never entrusting to a larger unit what can better be realised by a smaller one' (Spicker, 1991, pp. 3–4). Stuart Holland has expressed a similar optimism, in placing subsidiarity as the fulcrum in his blueprint for a more socially and economically coordinated Union, which, he suggests, could then be characterised by 'productive decentralisation' (Holland, 1993, pp. 16–17, 128–55).

The Treaty itself, however, as we have already emphasised, is more ambiguous. The inclusion of two implicitly rival definitions of subsidiarity in the same Treaty text leaves the precise meaning of the concept 'fatally confused' (Teasdale, 1993). The subsidiarity introduced in Articles A and B of the Treaty suggest a decentralising definition, where decisions in the Union are to be taken 'as closely as possible' to the citizen. Article 3B, however, establishes a procedural device for dividing competences between the Union and the member states, which is, according to such as John Peterson, 'undeniably' federal and centralist in ambition. This ambiguity is the conscious result of political expediency. Such an ambiguity, as we have already seen, means that subsidiarity can quite easily mean anything to anybody. Legal commentators have, interestingly, tended to favour a decentralising, pluralist, definition of subsidiarity. Nicholas Emiliou has championed subsidiarity as a mechanism for 'diversification', albeit in a recognisably federal European state (Emiliou, 1992). Most recently Ian Harden, whilst recognising that subsidiarity is more a 'recognition' of a need than a 'specific principle', suggests that it encapsulates the spirit of a plural, participatory democracy. It is, he says, 'not just about the relationship between States and the Union, but also about the search for a richer variety of collectivities, political and otherwise, which individuals can use as a meaningful context for their actions.' In such a way, the Union might be constituted by 'institutions with different, separate, forms of accountability, appropriate to their specific tasks' (Harden, 1994, pp. 613, 620, 624).

A related problem is the uncertainty as to how such a seemingly abstract and ill-defined constitutional mechanism could be applied in the concrete social and political situation. Industrial democracy, as a form of participatory democracy, might be one such application. Subsidiarity might be interpretable as a governing principle which can be extended to the workplace, founded in the Union constitution. Unfortunately, one immediate problem is that the legal status of subsidiarity, and the extent of its application, remain uncertain (Toth, 1994). In an intriguing discussion of the potential development of social policy in post-Maastricht Europe, Paul Teague has suggested how a decentralising determination of subsidiarity might reverse what he calls the 'co-ordination deficit' in current European industrial relations. Subsidiarity might be used to reintroduce a kind of European Union social contract, devolving both rights and responsibilities back to the individual worker. Whether this will actually happen, he concedes, is another matter (Teague, 1993, pp. 164–70). Certainly, the idea of a 'social dialogue' has been elevated to the status of something of an icon in contemporary Union ideology. According to Barry Fitzpatrick, the reintroduction of the dialogue in Articles 3 and 4 of the Social Policy Agreement, read in the light of the governing principle of subsidiarity, has 'greatly strengthened' the possibility of effecting a real dispersal of industrial power (Fitzpatrick, 1992, pp. 201, 207–8). Similarly, Clare McGlynn has suggested that the recent refining of the European Works Council directive (94/95), can be seen as a step, albeit small, in the direction of enhanced industrial and participatory democracy, founded on the subsidiarity principle (McGlynn, 1995). The possibilities for a genuinely plural and participatory democracy in the post-Maastricht industrial setting, at least, are certainly tangible. Of course, whether there is a corresponding political will is an entirely different question, and one to which we shall return in the final part of this chapter.

2 CITIZENSHIP

The second preconception which I want to challenge is citizenship. As with the so-called 'democratic deficit', there has been much talk about the need to enhance our sense of belonging to the Union, and the importance of impressing the idea of a 'people's Europe'. Citizenship appeared to be the solution, and so was duly presented as a centrepiece of the Maastricht Treaty. Once again, however, it was a very particular idea of political citizenship which was written into the European constitution. There are three particular preconceptions written into the Treaty determination of citizenship. First, Article 8 stipulates that the status of 'citizen of the Union' shall only be extended to persons 'holding the nationality of a Member State'. This determination has a number of repercussions. Most importantly, it is in the gift, ultimately, of the nation-states, and not the Union. As Carlos Closa has observed, the 'reliance of citizenship of the Union on nationality reflects merely the subordination of the Union to its Member States' (Closa, 1994, p. 119). The Treaty does not seem either able or willing to create a non-nationality idea of citizenship. A second related preconception is that Article 8B assumes that one of the defining assets of this political citizenship will be the entrenched right to partake in a representative democracy. We have already suggested that this itself is something of an arguable virtue. There is no right to partake in any other form of democracy in Article 8.

The third preconception is again related to the supposed rights which flow from this idea of citizenship. Article 8 also stipulates that the new citizens 'shall enjoy the rights conferred by this Treaty and shall be subject to the duties imposed thereby'. What this means, in effect, is that only those who are subject to the laws of the Community, the only justiciable part of the new Union, will enjoy the 'rights' of citizenship. This, it has been suggested, makes a 'mockery' of the entire idea of citizenship in the new Union (Anderson et al., 1994, pp. 106, 118). These laws are, of course, in the main part predominantly economic laws. Citizenship in the new Europe, as John Grahl and Paul Teague have reminded us, is not just political. It is a political concept founded upon a particular economic ideology (Grahl & Teague, 1994). Such a determination has all sorts of fairly obvious, and undesirable, consequences for those marginalised by this ideology. Two such groups, in particular, are migrant workers and the unemployed. Migrant workers have been consistently denied political or legal recognition in the Community. As we shall see in the next chapter, the Schengen and Dublin agreements with regard to the application of the free movement provisions to migrant workers were shamefully inadequate, and, as David O'Keeffe observed, merely served to underline the nascent xenophobia of the nation-states (O'Keeffe, 1992, pp. 12–19). The spirit of Schengen was prevalent at Maastricht (O'Keeffe, 1994). The only conclusion, as Hans D'Oliveira notes, is that the new Europe 'seems to fear its citizens as much as it fears uncontrolled migration, and makes clear again that, whatever the name, it is still an overwhelmingly economic enterprise' (D'Oliveira, 1994, p. 278).

The 'unemployed' fall into three categories. First, there are those who are tangibly unemployed, around 15–16 million of them, or nearly 12 per cent of the new citizenship (Wise & Gibb, 1993, pp. 206–9; Close, 1995, pp. 34–5). These are just those who would like to 'work'. They are constructively excluded from the 'rights' of citizenship. Second, there are those, many of whom are women, who work part-time and therefore continue to exist in a kind of limbo, still devoid, even after Maastricht, of the same kind of economic rights as the full-time worker. Thirdly, there are those, many of whom are, once again, women, who can be euphemistically termed 'voluntarily' unemployed, in that their form of work, often familial in nature, is not recognised as 'work' in European law (Ackers, 1994; Scheiwe, 1994). All in all, the Community, as Stuart Holland alleges, has created an economic 'underclass' of the unemployed and impoverished, with one in six European citizens officially surviving below the poverty line, and now effectively marginalised, not merely from work, but from the Union itself (Holland, 1993, p. 125).

Citizenship does not have to be politically and economically determined. There are alternatives. One such alternative, which has been increasingly advocated, is for a concept of citizenship founded instead upon a human rights determination. In the opinion of Siofra O'Leary,

> the establishment of a connection between the Community's commitment to fundamental rights and Community citizenship could promote the protection of individual rights as one of the central objectives of Community law and might help displace nationality as the single most important condition for the full enjoyment of Community citizenship. (O'Leary, 1995, pp. 542–3)

In this way, she adds perceptively, both citizenship and human rights relatedly defined could help to nourish a Community identity which is so clearly lacking at present (ibid., pp. 552–3). Rainer Bauboeck has suggested that the Community must underpin its concept of citizenship by a real commitment to 'both egalitarianism and universalism of citizen rights'. There must, he urges, be a 'transformation' of citizen rights into human rights (Bauboeck, 1991, pp. 30–1, 37). Article 8 waxes majestically on the subject of citizens' 'rights', and the same preconception applies. These so-called rights are determined solely as economic rights. Not only need this not be so, but jurisprudentially it can be argued that such rights are not rights in any meaningful sense of the word at all. Most obviously, in a Kantian sense, for example, all rights in any community must be universal, and founded upon the twin constituents of freedom and equality (Ward, 1993). The new European Union is still very far short of anything approaching such a principled or ethically based theory of rights. As we shall see in chapter 8, it is just as far short of anything approaching a genuine human rights foundation, and this is as much the case after Maastricht as before (Twomey, 1994, p. 121). In the absence of anything more solid, the European Court has intermittently sought recourse to the European Convention on Human Rights. However, the residual authority of member state courts to effect the Convention, as Koen Lenaerts notes, negates any possibility of it providing a universal source of principled 'rights' (Lenaerts, 1991, pp. 373–6). The Court itself has attempted to establish some sort of human rights jurisprudence, but, once again, the effect has been somewhat intermittent (Weiler, 1986). Its refusal to adopt a human rights jurisprudence in order to resolve certain high-profile 'law and morality' cases, such as *Grogan*, has rightly led to the accusation that it does not 'take rights seriously' (*Grogan*; cf. Phelan, 1992; Coppel & O'Neill, 1992).

A human rights foundation is not the only alternative determination of citizenship. Another more recent, though less persuasive, alternative is Ernest Wistrich's suggestion that citizenship could be extended to all those who pay taxes. Although he suggests that this would be more compatible on human rights terms, it is hard to see how it takes citizenship away from an economic basis. Wistrich's definition of human rights extends only so far as human rights of 'free movement' (Wistrich, 1994, pp. 78–94). A more promising approach is taken by Paul Close. Echoing Stuart Holland's observation, Close notes the effective exclusion from Union citizenship of an economic 'underclass'. This, he adds, reflects the feeling predominant in many of the member states, most obviously perhaps the UK, during the 1980s, where citizenship became consciously defined as something that had to be earned, as opposed to something to which people were entitled as of right (Close, 1995, pp. 45–52, 189–91). This, Close suggests, is the established definition of 'national' citizenship (ibid., pp. 55–81). The alternative model, which Close suggests might be particularly appropriate to the new Europe, is 'social' citizenship, founded on the 'democratic socialist' model articulated by a number of continental European political parties and commentators, and found, to a certain extent at least, in the Scandinavian corporatist model.

Such models are, he adds, 'pluralist' in nature, because they recognise the centrality of community and group interest, rather than merely concentrating citizenship on the status of the individual. The centrepiece of 'social' citizenship is the right to welfare provision, as opposed to welfare in the gift of the state (ibid., pp. 193–5). Rather than merely adopting the Scandinavian model, European Union 'social' citizenship is more likely to emerge as a kind of 'hybrid', part-Scandinavian and part-conservative–corporatist, as favoured in both Germany and France. The latter being occupationally-linked, though not purely employment-linked (ibid., pp. 203–22). Such an idea of citizenship must constantly guard against the danger of becoming too occupationally based, and, of course, too nationality based. However, it does offer the possibility of effecting a complementary citizenship for a new 'pluralist' Union. Such rights would be extended to group personalities, so that rights existed in both the individual and in communities and interest groups. It would, he concludes, be an idea of citizenship geared to participatory, as opposed to purely representative, democracy (ibid., pp. 242–68).

The issue of citizenship is, of course, inextricably linked with that of participatory democracy. The nexus has always been central in pluralist thinking. The nature of citizenship lay at the heart of Laski's idea of the pluralist state. As far as Laski was concerned, Aristotle's idea of citizenship was still valid. Citizenship is the ability to be ruled and to rule. If one is subject to the law, then one has the right to make the law and to do so immediately, as opposed to remotely, and only through the complexities of representative government. Laski advocated an 'ethical foundation' to citizenship, which he then extended to include various social rights, and concluded with an idea of citizenship which bears a close resemblance to the rhetoric of the Commission, if not the reality of the new European Union (Hirst, 1993, pp. 184–92). A definition of citizenship was at once a definition of right and of government. As he comments, in *The Foundations of Sovereignty*:

> For the duties of citizenship cannot be fulfilled, save under certain conditions; and it is necessary to ensure the

> attainment of those conditions against the encroachments of authority. I cannot here attempt any sort of detail; but it is obvious enough that freedom of speech, a living wage, an adequate education, a proper amount of leisure, the power to combine for social effort, are all of them integral to citizenship. They are natural rights in the sense that without them the purpose of the state cannot be fulfilled. They are natural also in the sense that they do not depend upon the state for their validity. They are inherent in the eminent worth of human personality. Where they are denied, the state clearly destroys whatever claims it has upon the loyalty of men. (ibid., p. 191)

This appeal for an alternative determination of citizenship and participatory governance has most recently found a voice in Dawn Oliver, who has seen the construction of the new Europe as the catalyst for a whole new debate. This, of course, is not to say that the Maastricht definition of citizenship is itself appropriate. On the contrary, it seems to be something of an 'afterthought'. However, it does highlight the historically contingent nature of liberal individual conceptions of citizenship, which have continued to be dominant in the member states. In an eloquent passage, she underlines its inadequacies:

> To define people as autonomous individuals in the Hayekian sense is to underestimate the extent to which we are, inevitably and indeed beneficially, dependent on one another. To define people as consumers and worker-producers is to undervalue their worth as individuals and the importance of the political process to good government. To undermine the role of the individual as a politically active participant in public decision-making is to give too much power to fallible officials. To neglect the importance of civic virtue is to risk the disintegration of civil society. (Oliver, 1994, p. 461)

It is, I would suggest, a salutary warning.

3 IDENTITY

What we are talking about here are really questions of identity. As Habermas emphasises, the questions of democracy and citizenship are always tied to issues of identity and nationalism. Democracy and citizenship are invariably, in modernist political thought, used to justify or 'legitimate' the nation-state, and to identify it. In this way the nation-state has always sought to accommodate the immanent tension that lies between capitalism and democracy. The rawness of this tension is merely amplified in the putative European state (Habermas, 1992, pp. 1, 7–13). Rainer Bauboeck, in similar vein, has emphasised that a political definition of citizenship always presumes a nationality–homogeneity nexus. It thus 'reflects the imperative of cultural homogeneity'. This homogeneity, he continues, is always a charade, which exists solely in the 'ideologies' of 'dominant majorities' (Bauboeck, 1991, p. 28). Carlos Closa has taken the analysis of democracy, citizenship and identity one stage further, by emphasising the pivotal role of the law. European law, he suggests, plays an active and decisive role in providing this spurious legitimation. What is needed, he adds, is acceptance of an alternative approach which attempts to construct an ethic of 'solidarity', which can then 'develop' a complementary ethic of 'identity', which is not founded upon a spurious pretence of cultural homogeneity (Closa, 1995, pp. 508–9).

The acceleration towards further economic integration in Europe, from the mid-1980s, as I suggested earlier, has been accompanied by an increased determination to effect a complementary political integration. It is not that this desire has been countered by any particularly rampant Euro-scepticism, even in the UK. It is the sheer apathy of Europeans which has been most disturbing, at least for pro-integrationists. Soledad Garcia refers to the irreducible nexus between 'legitimation deficit' and interest deficit (Garcia, 1993, p. 3). There was a perceived need, in the words of Juliet Lodge, to 'personalize integration' (Lodge, 1993, pp. 377–8). It was this resultant anxiety which lay behind the various attempts of such as the Adonnino Committee to enhance a European identity, by means of European flags, anthems, even space stations. It has consistently been assumed that no one seems to care about Europe, or at least care enough, because European integration cannot be 'identified' with anything. Neither the Community nor the Union appears to enjoy an identity. This is not to say that Europe does not enjoy an identity. This is the real problem. Europe already does enjoy an identity. Not only this, it is an identity which, as Jacques Derrida has recently reminded us, and as we saw in chapter 1, has always savoured and promoted heterogeneity. Europe, he suggests, is 'identified' by 'difference' (Derrida, 1992). The problem is thus compounded. Not only must the new Europe define itself, but it can only do so if it accommodates the reality of a Europe of 'differences' and provides political and social complements to such an identity.

As the 1980s progressed, the two things which it was hoped might inspire the new Europeans were the construction of a more democratic Europe, or at least one that appears to be more democratic, and the establishment of a European citizenship. Both, it was surmised, might encourage a feeling of belonging amongst the crushingly indifferent 'peoples' of Europe. However, as I have suggested above, the attempt to democratise the Union, and to establish citizenship, are far from satisfactory. The reason why they are unsatisfactory is that they presume some sort of European state, and so, as defining constituents of this state, they are themselves determined as concepts already familiar in the member states as mechanisms for establishing identity. Thus the democratising of Europe is presumed to mean the refining of a representative democracy, whilst European citizenship is a purely political-economic citizenship, founded upon the fiction of some sort of European nationality, aggregated from the nationality of the nation-states themselves. It is this assumption, that a more identifiable European 'state' would be a good thing, that is revealing. This is the fundamental preconception of modernity. It has always been one of the central tenets of pluralists, such as Laski and Cole, that 'states' are preoccupied by questions of identity. States wish to emphasise their definition as states, because it furnishes a sense of justification which otherwise does not exist. States are not natural entities. Thus, when we talk about questions of identity we are discussing the idea of states (Hirst, 1993, p. 76). More particularly, perhaps, we are talking about nation-states, because so many European states have embellished their self-justification on the premises of nationality.

There are then two possibilities. On the one hand, the 'new' Europe can continue to develop itself as a European state and try to create a complementary image. As Ernest Wistrich has recently suggested, it can continue in the spirit of the Adonnino Committee, sponsoring cycle races, youth orchestras, the free movement of fine art from museum to museum, and everything else which goes to embellish the mythology of the prosperous middle-class state. According to Wistrich, a 'European consciousness' will be most effectively realised by educational exchanges, presumably for those who are better educated, and a European TV station, so that, once again, presumably, citizenship will be graded according to the number of satellite stations each putative citizen can afford to subscribe to (Wistrich, 1994, pp. 87–94). Such an approach has its allurements. It is not confrontational, at least not as much as a radical overhaul of modern governance in Europe might be. It can also be done incrementally; a orchestra here, a cycle race there. But who is really going to be enthused by this Europe, except for the occasional nomadic trombone or piccolo player, and the millions of us who see in cycle racing the justification for social and political existence? Will this really effect a sense of 'belonging' to a more identifiable Europe?

Alternatively, if the European Union really wants somehow to create an identity for itself, it can do so by distancing itself, not only from the identities already enjoyed by Europe in its cultural and geographical sense, but also from the identities already established by the nation-states. If this is to be the case, and it is suggested that it is the only viable approach, there must be a radically alternative and distinguishable form of democracy in Europe, which does not presume the nationalistic qualities of representative democracy. Likewise there must be a radically different theory of citizenship, which is not based upon nationality, and is not something which can only be earned and enjoyed by those who submit to the pervasive economic and political ideology of the Union. Such a polity might describe or even define a different Europe. At the same time, it must be appreciated that any such putative European identity does not have to be, and indeed cannot be, in place of the established identity of Europe, or of its member states. There is no need for the European Union identity to be all-consuming, and it is futile to tilt at such a windmill. Any Union identity must exist alongside already pre-existing identities. If the Union can distance itself from the statist assumption that it can only assert itself by diminishing competing identities, then it can accept the reality of a multilayered Europe with a mosaic of different identities, not just regional, but social and functional, and so on. If it does this, then the new Europe can present itself as a political complement to the culturally and regionally heterogeneous Europe which is already 'identified'. A participatory and pluralist model of Union government, complemented by a non-exclusionary concept of social citizenship, might provide a means towards creating such an 'identity', but we can only make putative steps towards such a Europe if we rid ourselves of the preconceptions which dictate our present understanding of how identities must be shaped.

Part III

At the Margins of European Law

6 The Other Europeans

Not everybody in 'Europe' is a 'European', apparently. Millions of people – at a recent count in excess of nine million – live and work in the new Europe, but are denied the status of being 'European', normally because of their ethnic antecedents and the colour of their skin (Geddes, 1995, pp. 202–3). Certain antecedents and certain colours, in particular, are deemed to be inappropriate. These are not the sort of people that we want in the new Europe, save, that is, for their potential as immediate and ready candidates for economic exploitation. As Jürgen Habermas has recently emphasised, the marginalisation of groups of individuals, for variously spurious reasons, is the characteristic of the modernism and of the modern polity (Habermas, 1992). Nowhere are the margins of the new Europe more acutely revealed than in the exclusion of those who are defined as non-European. Of course, they are all European, but they are the 'other Europeans', those that fail the current political determination of what it is to be 'European'. What is particularly pertinent for us is the fact that the law plays a critical role in marginalising certain Europeans. The law, here, for millions of Europeans is the tool of their very real oppression. It is responsible, as I shall reveal in the first section of this chapter, not just for the inadequacies of its immigration, asylum and racial legislation, and for the related limitations of its free movement of persons provisions, but also in the wider sense, for the overarching constitutional failings, which contribute spectacularly to the law's overall inability to provide certain basic human and natural rights, rights which, I shall then suggest in the remaining sections of the chapter, are immanent to the human condition.

1 THE LAW OF BEING EUROPEAN

As I shall emphasise in the final section of this chapter, the legal determination of who is a European is intimately related not only to the questions of citizenship and to issues of nationality, but also to the often problematic implementation of legal measures to realise the cherished Community idol of the free movement of persons. Articles 48–66 of the Community Treaty provide for the free movement of workers, of the self-employed and of those who provide services. But not for anyone else. Moreover, in many areas, free movement is free in name only. Even the free movement of nationals has been frequently limited, most notoriously by the public policy, public security and public health exceptions in Article 48.3. What is politic, secure and healthy for the nationals of one member state is not necessarily so for another. The European Court's determination not to infringe upon domestic jurisdiction in this tender political area was revealed in the *Van Duyn* case, where the UK government was able to exercise its prerogative to exclude a member of the Church of Scientology (*Van Duyn*). In the subsequent *Rutili* case, the Court again reaffirmed that where there was no undue discrimination between workers, such as might effect a disequilibrium in the market between member states, domestic courts enjoy effective *carte blanche* in interpreting the free movement provisions (*Rutili*). It has rightly been questioned whether such an approach is in accord with the European Convention on Human Rights, and indeed, whether the free movement provisions can make sense if they are only couched in economic terms (Hall, 1991; Dallen, 1990, pp. 777–9).

More notorious still is the continued refusal to extend the right of free movement to non-EC migrant workers. Stuart Holland has emphasised the extent to which the EC has consistently marginalised the non-EC worker, and castigates it as one of the most 'regrettable' of 'social scars' (Holland, 1993, pp. 170–3). It is an anomaly demanded solely by national particularism. The continued member state determination of citizenship, as affirmed in the Maastricht Treaty, merely serves to exacerbate the anomaly (O'Keeffe, 1994, pp. 87–94). As David O'Keeffe suggests, as they stand, the Community free movement provisions merely serve to entrench a nation-state ethic of 'discrimination, racism and xenophobia and incitement to hatred and racial violence' (O'Keeffe, 1992, p. 19). It has become clear that the

Community's ambitions have outgrown the original Treaty provisions on free movement, not least in that they continue to act as a break on the effectiveness of the free market. The Commission has long recognised this, but has been unable to convince the nation-states that there would be sufficient economic gain to warrant such a symbolic relinquishment of sovereignty. Significantly, the proposal that free movement of qualified labour, in other words, that which is most economically viable, should be hastened, to the necessary exclusion of unskilled labour, reveals the real heartbeat of Commission ideology (Papandreou, 1990, pp. 197–202).

The European Court, perhaps unsurprisingly, has generally adopted an uneasy stance in the interpretation of the free movement provisions, wishing to articulate the spirit of the ideology without appearing to challenge member state jurisdiction (O'Keeffe, 1992). The nature of this unease was seen in the 1987 *Belgium* decision, where the Court decided that sporadic border controls were okay, but not systematic ones (*Belgium*; cf. O'Keeffe, 1992, pp. 9–10). Typically, and rather unhelpfully, the term 'worker' was not defined in the Rome Treaty, and much of the Court's energies have been devoted to providing an expansive definition in an effort to mitigate the rigours of the Treaty provisions. However, it has steadfastly adhered to a basic economic criterion for defining work, such that, in *Bettray*, for example, it refused to accept working for a drug rehabilitation scheme as an economically productive activity (*Bettray*). Similarly, in the determination of a worker's 'family', which under Regulation 1612/68 was intended to allow for the accompaniment of 'spouses and their descendants' and certain 'dependent relatives', the Court has interpreted the term to exclude mere cohabitees, whilst following suit, a domestic UK court has felt able to exclude those who subsequent divorce from workers (*Reed*; *Sandhu*). Most importantly of all, and most revealingly, when an alleged free movement right is even remotely perceived to be a threat to an economic objective, the Court has consistently suppressed the right. Thus in *Gebroeders Beentjes*, the Court allowed a contractor to evade related Community provisions designed to aid the movement of the long-term unemployed, in order to protect freedom of contract in the public procurement field (*Gebroeders Beentjes*).

The Schengen Agreement, which sought finally to abolish all border controls between the Benelux countries, France, Germany, Italy, Spain and Portugal, feinted to deceive. Moreover, as we shall see shortly, in its rigorous countermeasures against further immigration, the Agreement actually effects an increased atmosphere of intolerance and exclusion of others. In relation to the free movement of persons provisions, O'Keeffe rightly concludes that,

> it is ironic that the different initiatives to bring about the internal market and to realise the People's Europe thus far are characterised by an increase in the power of government to carry out checks and controls, to store and exchange information, while the judicial protection of the individual is, if anything, weakened. (O'Keeffe, 1992, p. 19)

As another commentator has similarly observed, the nation-states 'seem physically to panic at the sight of abolition of internal borders' (D'Oliveira, 1994, p. 278). Thus, all airports and seaports are still defined as external borders, and so is the Channel Tunnel, even though other railways are not. It is both absurd and irrational, aside from being in fundamental opposition to the overarching ideology of free movement. As D'Oliveira suggests, there is only one possible conclusion: 'The European Community seems to fear its citizens as much as it fears uncontrolled migration, and makes clear again that, whatever the name, it is still an overwhelmingly economic enterprise' (ibid.).

So much for those already 'in' the Community. But what of those 'outside', who would like to get 'in'? The state of immigration and asylum procedures in the new Europe is scandalous. Numerous provisions are alleged to be in breach of both the European and UN Conventions on human and civil rights. This situation has been exacerbated, both after the Schengen and Dublin Conventions and in the light of the Maastricht Treaty. In the latter, immigration and asylum were consigned to the so-called third 'pillar', justice and home affairs, and thus exist in a kind of non-justiciable twilight world, beyond the reach of human rights law, both as it stands in the Community, and in the wider world. Article

K gives the Council sole right to determine whether to grant the European Court jurisdiction over any Convention (Spencer, 1995, chs. 1–2; O'Keeffe, 1995, pp. 25–7). It is, however, the Schengen and Dublin Conventions which perhaps give most cause for concern. The potential abolition of internal borders engendered a complementary determination to strengthen external borders. 'Fortress Europe' was reinforced so as to repel all potential boarders (Geddes, 1995, pp. 214–15).

The focus at Schengen noticeably shifted from free movement to control (ibid., p. 210). This is perhaps best symbolised by the Schengen Information Service (SIS), the perceived 'backbone' of the Convention, which coordinates data-holdings on migrants, and immigrant and asylum-seekers (Baldwin-Edwards, 1991, pp. 208–9). Although, at first, the SIS failed to account for at least 50 per cent of such seekers, because it was restricted to a Latin-only alphabet, the establishment of the system was still widely condemned as a breach of civil liberties and contrary to the European Convention. It has even been suggested that the entire Schengen 'package' may be in breach of Community law itself in many related civil liberties areas (Spencer, 1995, pp. 55–9; O'Keeffe, 1991). Similar criticisms have been repeatedly made of the Convention's narrow determination of 'family', the penalisation of illegal crossing of borders, visa requirements and data exchange and policing (O'Keeffe, 1992, pp. 14–16). The Meijers Commission made five essential criticisms of the Schengen Convention; (1) that it lacked parliamentary or judicial control, (2) that there was no reference to the European Convention, (3) that the asylum provisions fell well short of the standards prescribed in the Geneva Convention, (4) that the member states gained enhanced control of data relating to their own citizens, and (5) that the governing Schengen Executive Committee was unacceptably secretive and unaccountable. The lack of openness with regard to the execution of the Schengen procedures is seen by a number of commentators as one of the most blatant regressions from the principle of democratic governance in the present Union (Curtin & Meijers, 1995).

Immigration and asylum provisions in the new Europe remain essentially in the preserve of the nation-states, both individually and in their intergovernmental capacity. Schengen did nothing to mitigate this. On the contrary it positively reinforced member state jurisdiction. This is very much a response to the sensitivities of the member states, all of whom are defensive of their rights with regard to the immigration and asylum policy, albeit to different degrees. The 1993 Commission Report, following the Maastricht Treaty Declaration on Asylum advised the pressing need for harmonisation of asylum laws, but then concluded lamely that it recognised that political considerations meant that the 'time is not yet right' (Spencer, 1995, pp. 83–5). Not that the Commission's apparent concern for harmonisation was driven by any ethical distaste for the inconsistencies and injustices effected by fragmented immigration policies. Harmonisation, it has been consistently suggested, is necessary for the sake of the internal market. In contrast, it is clear, and was made particularly clear by the Dublin Convention, that harmonisation is not, at least for the member states, a governing principle.

As far as it is at all concerned, Union immigration and asylum policy is primarily geared to controlling, or more accurately negating, migration flows. The redefinition of asylum-seekers to exclude 'economic refugees' is merely the most obvious mechanism by which to effect wholly spurious exclusion measures (D'Oliveira, 1994, pp. 265–9). In 1980, 65 per cent of asylum-seekers were granted access to the Community. In 1990, that figure was reduced to just 10 per cent (Baldwin-Edwards, 1991, p. 200). The trend amongst individual member states has seen an alarming increase in forced deportations, particularly amongst the Mediterranean countries: Spain, Italy and Greece (ibid., p. 201). The extra-judicial deportation of Albanians from Italy is only the most notorious documented example (Nascimbene, 1992, pp. 719–20). A rather less well-known, but equally revealing, measure, is the Commission's policy for 'stimulating and facilitating' the return of African nationals (O'Keeffe, 1995, p. 31). The spirit of deportation is very much at the heart of Community immigration ideology. Although there are related provisions for the expedited return of unskilled migrants to Poland, there do not seem to be any comparable measures for the expedited or 'stimulated' return of skilled or wealthy immigrants with white skin (O'Keeffe, 1991, p. 195).

The refugee problem is a worldwide one. Between 1970 and 1994, the number of refugees increased nearly tenfold, from around 2.5 million to 23 million, to which can be added 26 million other displaced persons. The new Europe provides asylum sanctuary for just 6000 (Spencer, 1995, p. 76). Without doubt, this is the 'decade of the migrant' (Husbands, 1992, p. 276). Immigration is, of course, a byproduct of the 'success' of the common market. With each year the polarisation of economic wealth and resources, across both the Community and the continent itself, increases (Geddes, 1995, pp. 200–2). In the face of the perceived invasion of Europe by the newly freed, if somewhat impoverished and undernourished, migrant, in 1992 Community Immigration Ministers approved emergency measures deliberately designed to expedite further various mechanisms for refusing entry for immigrant applicants. With regard to refugees, the Ministers decided that all 'manifestly unfounded' applications could be immediately rejected without appeal, and furthermore, that neither famine nor war conditions could themselves qualify as 'founded'. Member states were under a Community obligation immediately to expel all failed applications. Moreover, in contravention of the European Convention, and in blatant disregard for any other familiar and reasonable civil liberties provisions, it added that member states should enjoy the 'power in appropriate circumstances to restrict the personal liberty of people liable to expulsion' (Spencer, 1995, pp. 87–90). This supremely defensive attitude is reinforced by a series of revealing complementary provisions, such as the tightening of carrier sanctions and the 'one application only' procedure for asylum-seekers (ibid., pp. 91–4).

One of the most undesirable, and most predictable, outcomes of such an attitude has been the tangible increase in racism and xenophobia within the Community, partly the cause of tolerating nation-state primacy in the field of race discrimination legislation and partly the cause of the Community's own legal impotence (O'Keeffe, 1995, pp. 32–3; Geddes, 1995, pp. 198–200, 211–14). Community anti-racist measures are notoriously slack, being, as Spencer notes, a series of 'sonorous but largely meaningless pronouncements', in the form of institutional declarations (Spencer, 1995, pp. 131–2). Instead of combating racism, the European constitution encourages a culture of exclusion, which is somehow 'justified' by the presence of legal measures which seek to define ever more clearly those who are not acceptable as putative members of the new Europe (ibid., p. 105). The situation is not helped by the prevailing assertion that immigration is somehow a 'problem'. Foreigners are a 'problem', as far as the Union is concerned. Such an attitude can only serve to lend a spurious degree of legitimacy to extreme right-wing racist policies towards forcible repatriation, and so on (Geddes, 1995, p. 207). Even the Commission has recently acknowledged that racism and xenophobia are a threat, not necessarily to the moral well-being of the new European citizen, but, far more importantly, to the economic efficiency of the internal market (Geddes, 1995, p. 213).

This exclusion is further exacerbated by the internalisation of marginalisation. Those who enter the new Europe, as immigrants, are socially and economically marginalised. As the Commission itself recognised, economic poverty is immediately translated into social deprivation. Immigrants are consciously channelled into a kind of Community subspecies, which has all the anticipated wider cultural effects:

> If today's immigrants were left to fend for themselves they would continue to occupy the bottom rungs of society. . . . The larger surrounding society turns hostile, develops rejection and stigmatisation mechanisms and resorts to uncivilised policing, thus reinforcing the vicious circle of exclusion breeding marginalisation. (Spencer, 1995, p. 109)

Yet, the Commission's own 1991 report on immigration shared all the populist xenophobic rhetoric. It created images of 'floods' of immigration, and referred to asylum procedures as being 'increasingly used by potential emigrants for purposes other than those for which they were originally designed', and 'swamped by persons seeking the social rights . . . granted to asylum applicants but no longer being granted in other cases as a consequence of the halting of economic immigration'. As Michael Spencer has noted, it is one thing for there to be a popular misconception about the dangers of immigration, but it is quite another for an institution of the Community to encourage xenophobia (ibid., pp. 109–10).

In the absence of harmonisation, immigration and asylum provisions continue to vary hugely from one member state to another (Baldwin-Edwards, 1991, pp. 203–7). The UK has always been the most consistently defensive, and insisted on the General Declaration inserted in the Single European Act, which reserved member state exclusive competence on immigration matters. It is, of course, as much a symbolic defence. Electorates, it is assumed, are reassured that people from different ethnic backgrounds can be excluded from the UK. The irony is that the determination to make a show of rigorous immigration barriers merely encourages illegal immigration and actually increases the disruptive economic effects of migration flow (Sciortino, 1991). The absurdity of the resultant Community situation was revealed in the so-called Bangemann 'wave', which effected a compromise whereby EC nationals were obliged to wave their passports at immigration officials, who, however, were not allowed to insist upon them being opened for inspection (Spencer, 1995, pp. 51–2). In the more recent past, the Commission has revealed an increased awareness of the wider repercussions of the present fragmented and fundamentally unjust state of European immigration policy, acknowledging with something of an understatement that immigrants 'can be subject to exploitation and be in an extremely vulnerable position' (ibid., pp. 114–15). The European Parliament has robustly criticised the continuing inconsistencies resulting from the maintenance of member state jurisdiction in the area of immigration and asylum, in the wake of both Schengen and the Maastricht Treaty. Its van Outrive Report concluded:

> For the moment, the Member States are in the ascendent in their long-standing rivalry with the Commission. The introduction of the third pillar is evidence of this. It ought to be realised that much power is being transferred to national officials. This is a threat to a democratic Europe; it definitely represents a step backwards and cannot be accepted without protest. (ibid., p. 64)

However, despite such rhetorical awareness, the fact remains that the new Europe remains impotent in the face of the nation-states, and thus by a constructive sin of omission equally as responsible for the marginalisation and social and economic injustices which result. It seems that there is a real danger that the objectives which drive the completion of the internal economic market have resulted in a very real derogation from basic principles of human rights with regard to immigration and asylum procedures (Geddes, 1995, pp. 214–15; O'Keeffe, 1992, p. 14). Only with the recognition of a human rights foundation in Community law, and with the jurisdiction of this foundation extended to include immigration and asylum procedures, can these derogations be amended (Spencer, 1995, p. 217; O'Keeffe, 1991, pp. 217–19). The justiciability issue is of paramount importance. The impotence and timidity of the European Court, as notoriously revealed in the *Demirel* case, can lead to what one recent commentary has termed 'quite horrible consequences'. In this case it led to forcible expulsion and repatriation, and the destruction of the supposedly revered 'family nexus' (*Demirel*; cf. Scott, 1992).

2 OTHERNESS

As I suggested above, marginalisation has been termed the characteristic of modernism. According to Jürgen Habermas, modernity is the obsession with determining identities, of defining self and other (Habermas, 1992). It is not therefore surprising that the problem of 'otherness' has emerged as one of the essential questions in critical and post-modern political theory. In a recent essay Julia Kristeva has emphasised that the critical question of 'otherness' is intimately bound up with the question of nationality. In 'What of Tomorrow's Nation?', Kristeva impresses the extent to which the post-modern era is the product of the 'crisis' of identity. The search for origins and identity, she adds, has become particularly acute in the disturbingly fragmented and alienating world of the twentieth century. The search for identity is always, in her words, a 'hate reaction', a determination to isolate, exclude and oppress others. Thus, in turn, as that search is all the more frenetic today, then it is not surprising that the 'hate reaction' is all the deeper (Kristeva, 1993, pp. 1–5). In order to defuse such a reaction, we must come to understand and define ourselves as 'other'. Otherness, she impresses, is the only universal' (ibid., p. 21). As she continues:

> I am convinced that, in the long run, only a thorough investigation of our remarkable relationship both with the *other* and *strangeness within ourselves* can lead people to give up hunting for the scapegoat outside their group. (ibid., pp. 50–1)

This thesis, of course, chimes with a number of fellow critics. Derrida has likewise emphasised that we are all 'others', all particular, all different and all, to some degree, excluded from one another. According to Derrida the essence of jurisprudence, and of ethics, is the deconstruction of universalism and the recognition of universal particularism (Derrida, 1990). Moreover, it is not just critical philosophy which has embraced such a thesis. It is also a theme central to much twentieth-century literature. Thus, most famously, Albert Camus's *The Outsider* graphically portrays the essence of 'otherness' in Mersault's coming to appreciate that he, like the Arab he kills, is destined to be excluded, to be an outsider.

The essence of modernity according to Kristeva is the determination to train nationalism in the cause of the nation-state. The mechanism for this training is the concept of citizenship, which was geared, in the Enlightenment vision, towards 'politicising nationalism'. In a sense it is a case of letting the cat out of the bag. The humanist ambition of modernity acknowledged the 'moral' duty of recognising the other. This she applauds. The 'recognition of otherness', she affirms, 'is a right and a duty for everyone.' It was the attempt to define citizenship in terms of the nation-state, in 'opposition' to the wider world, which was flawed. Rather than being in opposition to others, citizenship should be seen as a complement to Enlightenment cosmopolitanism, and national identity should stand without the assertion of nation-state and nationalist primacy. In support of her thesis, Kristeva invokes the authority of Montesquieu's '*esprit générale*', and his theory of private right protected by public law but prior to it (Kristeva, 1993, pp. 25–37). Montesquieu, she emphasises, recognised that man is man before he is a citizen. That is not to say that he is a particular type of man; such a determination can only be a 'self'-determination (ibid., pp. 61–3). Montesquieu is not a lone authority. Habermas cites Rousseau in the same way in order to make the same point (Habermas, 1992, pp. 3–4).

Another candidate is Immanuel Kant. Kant's theory of law has often been cited as a model for both international human rights and, more immediately, for the new Europe (Thompson, 1992, chs. 2, 4–5). The virtue of using a Kantian model is enhanced by a proper appreciation of his theory, not just of public international and cosmopolitan law, but also of private law. The importance of private law lies in the emphasis upon right as an integral quality to the human condition. Kantian right is founded upon freedom, just as Kantian reason is founded upon the 'moral law within'. The twin concepts are crucially immanent within the individual. In the *Groundwork* he emphasised that freedom is not merely theoretical, but actual as well, and could thus provide the core of a universal ethics founded upon a concept of reciprocal duty. At the same time, in the *Critique of Judgement*, the *Critique* all too often ignored by legal philosophers, Kant accommodated the individual and difference, and accounted for this difference with the concept of judgement. Individuality, he emphasised, was the essence of humanity and in politics always enjoyed dominion over universality. The accommodation of the individual in a community was revealed most strikingly in sections 21 and 40 of the *Critique*, in the form of the '*sensus communis*' as an idea of communicative rationality. Here Kant most explicitly reconciled the existence of the 'other':

> we must include the idea of a sense common to all i.e. of a faculty of judgment which, in its reflection, takes account (*a priori*) of the mode of representation of all other men in thought, in order, as it were, to compare its judgment with the collective reason of humanity. . . . This is done by comparing our judgment with the possible rather than the actual judgments of others, and by putting ourselves in the place of any other man, by abstracting from

> the limitations which contingently attach to our judgment. (Kant, 1991, p. 151)

It was in the light of *The Groundwork* and the *Critique of Judgement* that Kant turned to constructing his *Metaphysics of Morals,* where right was again immanent and reciprocal. The right of the self was determined by precisely the same right of the other. Conceptually, right is indivisible. This is the essence of private right; a complement to, not a derogation from, the particularity and subjectivity of the individual (cf. Ward, 1994d).

By her own admission the essence of Kristeva's thesis owes much to Hannah Arendt. Moreover, it can be no coincidence that so much of Arendt's work on exclusion and 'otherness' should owe so much to Kant, and particularly to the *Critique of Judgement* and the *Metaphysics of Morals.* In her *Lectures on Kant's Political Philosophy* she ascribes her entire complementary theory of 'participatory democracy' to Kant's later political writings (Arendt, 1982). Arendt is one of the most influential theorists of the 'other'. She, perhaps better than most, appreciated the plight of the outsider. Following Kant, freedom remained at the very heart of all her writings, as the foundation for self-determination and emancipation (Heller & Feher, 1988, pp. 89–105). The strongest theoretical statements on 'otherness' undoubtedly come out in her three-volume *Origins of Totalitarianism,* in which she decried the dangerous 'tyranny of consensus'. The distinction clearly drawn in *Origins* lies between totalitarianism and pluralism; the former excludes certain others, the latter includes all as other. In the opening volume, *Antisemitism,* she identified Nazism as the epitome of anti-pluralism, and illustrated the phenomenon of exclusion with reference to the infamous Dreyfus case. The philosophical complement to the Dreyfus case, and to all such occurrences of anti-Semitic activity, she asserted, was the supranationalism which seeks to destroy community justice (Arendt, 1951a, pp. 5, 91–120). Her use of a trial scenario as the apogee of excluding otherness is of course instructive. She had used exactly the same scenario in her accout of Eichmann's trial, and of course it was precisely that used by Camus (Arendt, 1963). Foucault, similarly, emphasised how much the institutions of the law serves to justify the exclusion of the 'others' from society (Foucault, 1979).

The same theme was developed in volume two, *Imperialism*, which castigated the rise of imperialism as a supranational force nourished by nationalism and destructive of both community and individual. The politics of national citizenship represented the triumph of 'legal mysticism' (Arendt, 1951b, pp. 4, 19–37, 115–17, 123–5, 166–82). In the final volume, *Totalitarianism*, Arendt returned to Nazism, together with Stalinism, and castigated their triumphs as representing the 'mass atomisation' of the 'doomed man', alienated from the community, and thus alienated from the distinguished 'other'. Ultimately, 'total domination', she suggested, will always try 'to organise the infinite plurality and differentiation of human beings as if all humanity were just one individual'. The exclusion of the other from the legal process was always the first symbolic step, because the taking away of legal rights from any individual represented the removal of legal rights from all. The ambition of totalitarianism and nationalism is first to 'kill the juridical person in man' (Arendt, 1951c, pp. 1–4, 21–8, 91–2, 136, 145). The only philosophical justification for law was the Kantian; jurisprudence based on immanent morality and reciprocal individual duty (Arendt, 1951c, pp. 158–68; cf. Canovan, 1992, pp. 24–6).

This pervasive concern with marginalisation and the definition and exclusion of others has not, of course, gone unnoticed by critical legal theorists. Allan Hutchinson has written persuasively on the need for society to readmit those it excludes, not just legally, but politically and economically as well. His solution, like so many, is the recognition of individuality in a participatory democracy that denies 'the existence' of any 'inside/outside limits' (Hutchinson, 1988, pp. 287–90). The wider problem of the alienated individual was recognised by Peter Gabel and Paul Harris, who suggested that the modern state sought to exclude internally the individual from power and from other individuals (Gabel & Harris, 1982, p. 371). Peter Gabel, because of his particular engagement with the continental tradition in critical philosophy, has emerged as one of the most critically aware in relation to the exclusion of individuals both within and without determined communities. The problem of modernity, he recognised, was the problem of 'boundaries' of pretended 'legitimation' (Gabel, 1980, pp. 25–7). The bestowal of citizenship and rights, he observed perceptively, was in fact a conscious attempt to encourage communities to exclude individuals, and citizenship was, thus, the key component of marginalisation (Gabel, 1984). In his celebrated engagement with Duncan Kennedy, Gabel again emphasised the role that law can play in legitimating the marginalising of 'others', whilst disguising the reality that we are all others, mutually dependent and co-determinative (Gabel & Kennedy, 1984, pp. 44–54). On the same theme, Jerry Frug has emphasised the particular potential for labour and economic law to exploit the marginalised and disempowered (Frug, 1987, p. 559). The other can only be empowered, according to Frug, by the radical decentralisation of adminstrative power, thus enhancing the possibilities of a plural and participatory community (Frug, 1990, pp. 574–86).

3 SOME CONCLUSIONS

As I suggested at the beginning of this chapter, and indeed in the previous chapter, the question of exclusion and inclusion of individuals within the Community is intimately bound up with the related issues of nationality and citizenship. Julia Kristeva sees the redetermination of national identity without nationalism as the best hope for a better future. Moreover, she sees the present evolution of the new Europe as a positive signpost. Not that the new Europe has yet abandoned its association of national identity with exclusionary citizenship and political nationalism, but she concludes:

> One can hope for the emergence of mature peoples who do not need a *someone* to represent or even state the principles of their identity. One can wish that the very idea of nation, saturated through the mingling of economies and cultures, might open up on other unions where the bond between human beings would be located, thus forcing political discourse to move away from national constraints. (Kristeva, 1993, pp. 75–6)

Citizenship in its modernist guise, as Siofra O'Leary has recently emphasised, is a designation of 'privilege' (O'Leary, 1995, pp. 540–1). It ensures the exclusion of others. As Joseph Weiler has eloquently observed, in today's European Community:

> Nationality as a referent for interpersonal relations, and the human alienating effect of *Us* and *Them* are brought back again, simply transferred from their previous intra-Community context to the new inter-Community one. We may have made little progress if the *Us* becomes a European (instead of a German or French or British) and the *Them* becomes those outside the Community or those inside who do not enjoy the privileges of citizenship. (Weiler, 1992, p. 68)

The possible solutions to our immediate problem of Europe's 'others' is, therefore, to a greater degree bound up with alternative models of citizenship. One of the more practical and immediately possible remedies would be the 'dilution' of the nationality–citizenship nexus. Alternative models of 'social citizenship', as articulated by such as Paul Close, would necessarily reduce the status of nationality as a criterion for inclusion and exclusion (Close, 1995). As Andrew Evans has implied, such a 'dilution' would itself be a crucial component in any political evolution beyond 'sovereignty' (Evans, 1991). Such a thesis is, of course, very much in line with the revered functionalist 'spillover' thesis so popular during the early decades of the Community. As we have already seen, it is along these lines that Carlos Closa has invoked a Habermasian 'solidarity' as the basis for a new non-nationality citizenship which would better effect a non-exclusionary Community (Closa, 1995, pp. 508–9). The pluralistic quality of such a polity, together with the practical essentiality of constitutional guarantees, is emphasised by Habermas himself, who concludes:

> The European states should agree upon a liberal immigration policy. They should not draw their wagons around themselves and their chauvinism of prosperity, hoping to ignore the pressures of those hoping to immigrate or seek asylum. The democratic right of self-determination includes, of course, the right to preserve one's own political culture,

which includes the concrete context of citizen's rights, though it does not include the self-assertion of a privileged cultural life form. Only within a constitutional framework of a democratic legal system can different ways of life coexist equally. These must, however, overlap within a political culture, which again implies an impulse to open these ways of life to others. (Habermas, 1992, p. 17)

This is, of course, the kind of polity articulated by a number of other advocates of 'solidarity'. Richard Rorty is one. Rorty's 'solidarity' is realised in a conversational community, in which all parties are not merely free to participate, but are active participants. Conversation, for Rorty, realises and empowers pluralism. Using the same term as Habermas, and interestingly echoing the later Rawls, Rorty refers to solidarity as the 'overlapping of vocabularies'. This juxtaposition, of solidarity, community and conversation, he terms 'postmodern bourgeois liberalism'. The 'private ironist', the hero of Rorty's new post-modern world, is precisely defined as the 'other' in a world populated solely by 'others'. As Rorty himself acknowledged, the 'private ironist' is the 'other' of Camus and Dostoevsky, Nabokov and Orwell (Rorty, 1989). As we have already seen, Rorty's 'solidarity' has been adopted by a number of critical legal scholars as a philosophical foundation for a juridical idea of participatory democracy (cf. Hutchinson, 1989). Moreover, Rorty himself has suggested that the kind of participatory democracy articulated by such as Roberto Unger is precisely the jurisprudential complement needed for a post-modern liberal community (Rorty, 1991, pp. 177–92). In turn, this is, of course, what was suggested by Hannah Arendt, who took the Kantian '*sensus communis*' and rewrote it in the language of participatory democracy (Arendt, 1972, pp. 231–3). We shall return to these models in the final chapter.

Ultimately, what is really being suggested here is an alternative post-modern conception of citizenship rooted in a comparable post-modern conception of human rights. The 'inclusion' of the other depends upon an acceptance of the ideas presented in the previous chapter, and indeed some of those which we shall consider subsequently in chapters 8 and 9. Such an understanding of human rights, in Rorty's opinion, will concentrate on redefining the 'human', rather than the 'right'. People, he suggests, must be 'respected' as people, and not as political components. We do not need to enjoy a common political identity to be human. Respect does not presume commonality. If there is no commonality, then there cannot be an identifiable body of excluded. Instead, echoing Kristeva, there is particularity, in which everyone is 'other', and no one is (Rorty, 1993, pp. 112–18). Such a vision chimes with that recently and forcefully articulated by Joseph Weiler. Whilst maintaining a deference to an essentially modernist conception, Weiler similarly talks of 'humaneness' and 'human dignity' as the proper foundations for human rights. In a specific critique of human rights and the status of non-EC nationals, he concludes: 'There is an inevitable violation of human dignity in a legal construct which insists on seeing an individual not as an end itself, but solely as a means and instrument at the service of other persons and other goals.' Commenting on the *Diatta* case, in which a divorced non-EC woman was stripped of her Community rights, he continues:

> in no situation can she be stripped of her humaneness. And it is that humaneness which guarantees her own fundamental rights. Under Community law she must be accepted not simply as a means to ensure free movement but as a person, a universe unto itself. Once an individual, for whatever reason or on whatever basis, comes within the field of application of Community law, his or her fundamental rights must be guaranteed. For the Court to say that at the moment of her divorce she does not only lose her derivative rights under Community law (which is acceptable), but also protection of fundamental human rights, is to strip her of humaneness. It is to acknowledge that under Community law she is a mere instrumentality. (Weiler, 1992, p. 90; cf. *Diatta*)

Theoretical models for alternative forms of citizenship and human rights which, in turn, would serve to reduce the exclusionary nature of the present European Union are fine, but only, of course, as theoretical models. Whether political reality will admit the demands of justice and equity by adopting an alternative model is less certain. Indeed, it might be said that the prospects are worse now than ever before. Certainly, that is the opinion of most commentators. But that should not stop us articulating with a consistent urgency the need to redefine the identity of being 'European' so as to admit all those who wish to aspire to the same quality of life that the new Europe is so proud to proclaim. In this sense the new Europe could be seen as a crucial component in the redefinition of 'otherness' across the world. A post-modern Europe could finally realise the ambition of effecting a society in which all inhabitants enjoyed private rights as a reality, not as a gift. As the the UN Commissioner for Refugees concluded, in 1992:

> As we move into the nineties there is no doubt that Europe is at a crossroads. Will Europe turn its back on those who are forced to move, or will it strengthen its long tradition of safeguarding the rights of the oppressed and the uprooted? Will Europe build new walls, knowing that walls did not stop those who were fleeing totalitarian persecution in the past? Or will Europe help to bridge the abyss which now separates East from West and North from South? Will Europe and the rest of the industrialised world have the courage to commit themselves politically and economically to attack severe poverty, underdevelopment and social injustice which leads to oppression, violence and displacement? The path which we follow will create the kind of world we bestow on future generations. (Spencer, 1995, pp. 98–9)

7 The Limits of Sex Equality Law in the New Europe

It has become almost commonplace now to establish sex equality as an unarguable good, and then to decry the failings of European law adequately to effect this good in the European Community. In this chapter I want to subvert these preconceptions, because, like all preconceptions, they are infinitely deconstructible, and their deconstruction, rather than threatening their veracity, can only serve to strengthen them. In the first part of the chapter, I want to introduce some of the basic tenets in contemporary feminist jurisprudence which have tended to enjoy dominion in the current debate surrounding the nature of sex equality in the Community. At the same time, I want to introduce an alternative, explicitly post-modern feminist approach which, I shall suggest, takes feminism well 'beyond' the now rather stale 'limits' of the sex equality debate. In the second part, I shall place this jurisprudence within the specific context of European Community law and suggest why the post-modern alternative might offer something more in the new Europe.

1 BEYOND THE SEX EQUALITY DEBATE

I do not intend here to dwell too long on the standard arguments surrounding what sex equality should mean or how substantive problems of inequality should be addressed. Indeed, one of the problems in current feminist jurisprudence is that the arguments are only too familiar. Like all discourses, the sex equality debate has been captured and objectified, the alternatives set in jurisprudential stone. This is not an error, because it was not something which could be avoided. The wisdom lies in knowing that all discourses are ultimately objectified and can only progress if their (pre)conceptions are subverted. However, at the risk of momentarily entrenching further the sanctification of this discourse, I shall briefly examine the arguments that need to be subverted, so that we can be better aware of what we are going to go 'beyond'.

At the same time, it must first be emphasised that there is no uniform feminist theory on sex equality, or for that matter any other issue. It is the perception that there might be which must be addressed. The pervasive argument in sex equality, until recent years at least, has been that of sameness and difference. The dominion that this debate enjoys, and the dangers which it poses, have been uncompromisingly articulated by Catherine MacKinnon. The sameness/difference debate, as MacKinnon suggests, gives women just two choices; they can either aspire to be the same as men and to enjoy the same rights, or they can campaign to have their difference from men recognised in law. Either way, women are compared with a male norm, and by presenting women with these two choices, and these two choices only, the debate immediately establishes parameters. Any such rights-based approach tends to be founded on 'a claim to similarity'. A collateral argument here is that the formal enactment of rights for women, aside from being made in a comparative sense, will not address in reality the myriad of substantive inequalities which women face. In other words, a liberal rights-based approach, and MacKinnon unsurprisingly cites Ronald Dworkin as the arch-exponent of such an approach in contemporary jurisprudence, actually serves to entrench the real inequalities which women encounter, and does more harm in practice than good. Thus, as MacKinnon concludes, the phrase 'sex equality law' contains three particular preconceptions. First, it assumes a particular determination of 'sex' as denoting difference. Second, it then presumes that any 'inequalities' must be the result of 'mistakes' in addressing difference. Third, 'law' explicitly assumes that the problem is something that can somehow be resolved by law (MacKinnon, 1989).

What we are really talking about, rather than sameness or difference, is questions of power, and MacKinnon has developed her critique along these lines in her more recent writings, suggesting that, in place of sameness/difference, a more critical legal approach should be adopted concentrating on confronting more immediate inequalities in practical terms (MacKinnon, 1991). What can be seen most clearly during the 1990s is an intensification of concern in the politics of law. It can almost be termed an anti-philosophical backlash. The enthusiasm for 'critical' legal feminism is a testimony to this impulse. One who has allied this pragmatic impulse to an identifiable critical legal feminism is Deborah Rhode. Rhode urges the replacement of sameness/difference with a focus on 'disadvantage' (Rhode, 1989). Like MacKinnon, Rhode rejects what she calls 'liberal legalism' as represented in contemporary legal and political structures. Classical liberalism, she rightly suggests, is a predominantly economic ideology which sanctifies the role of the contract, both in public and private law guise, as the norm of 'affiliative' relationships. In place of such an abstract and mythological liberal ideology, she advocates the idea of 'social' relationships. In line with received CLS wisdom, she suggests that all 'choices' are ideologically charged and made in pervasively social settings (Rhode, 1990).

Where Rhode, interestingly, distinguishes critical legal feminism from CLS in general, and perhaps to a certain extent from such as MacKinnon, is in her approach to rights. Whilst challenging the nature of liberal, autonomous rights, she clings to an alternative theory, of socially constructed rights, which are thus better capable of reflecting the common 'lived experience' of women. Rights, she suggests, have a 'special resonance' and their presence or, indeed, potential as tools for improving the situation of women, cannot be denied (Rhode, 1990). Perhaps the most eloquent defence of such an approach is Patricia Williams. Williams clings to rights because, quite simply, it is the only game in town, and writing not just as a woman, but as a black woman, she can testify to the benefits which were accessed by black people in the US by litigating rights under the Constitution. She does not wish to 'idealize' rights, but neither does she wish to deconstruct them, for the sheer joy of deconstruction. Such an exercise can only serve the interest of women if it presents a viable and more effective alternative. The more deconstructive edge of CLS and feminist critical legal theory, she suggests, does not offer any such alternative. Rather like

Rhode then, Williams suggests that rights must be reconstructed or 'reconfigured' in a more 'civil' or 'societal', as opposed to individual, form, rather than simply abandoned (Williams, 1987). This is not a reactionary or even liberal approach. Such an assignation would be entirely to miss the point of Williams' critique. What it is, is a supremely pragmatic critique, and a supremely political one in its primarily strategic sense.

A similarly 'strategic' position has been taken by Diane Majury. The 'equality' debate, she acknowledges, is the dominant one, and so cannot be ignored. However, the welter of alternative equality 'models' presented by various feminist scholars militates against any objective determination of 'equality', either in theory or in practice. Moreover, echoing MacKinnon, she suggests that the 'equality' debate distracts us from appreciating the power(lessness) and (dis)advantage debates which more accurately reflect the deeper structures that underpin the real situation of women in contemporary society. The debate, she thus argues, must then be redirected towards 'inequality'. An 'inequality-based strategy' does not establish goals, but is, rather, directed towards addressing substantive and particular inequalities. (In)equality is thus a symbol of a strategy. Ultimately, this strategy must concentrate on enhancing the female discourse in a general sense, by encouraging dialogue and conversation between women, which can then contribute to the crystallising of women's 'interests'. What is implicit in this conclusion is the fact that equality is, in any situation, an intellectual fiction. There can be no single meaning of sex equality, because there is no single determination of women, as of course there is not of men. Different women must fight to establish their different particular determinations of equality (Williams, 1991). The first duty of the feminist legal thinker is not to pronounce on sex equality, or perceived inadequate approximations to it, but to radically destabilise any pretended determination of the idea, in practice or reality (Majury, 1991).

With Majury certainly, and to a lesser extent with Rhode and Williams also, we are witnessing the approaching influence of post-modernist thinking. CLS fell prey to the tempting of post-modernism by the late 1980s, and over the last few years an identifiable post-modern feminism has emerged from within critical legal feminism (Rhode, 1990; cf. Goodrich, 1992). As Joan Williams has suggested, post-modernism offers a recourse 'beyond' any of the sameness/difference debates which pervade, not only feminism, but also related theories of exclusion, most obviously, perhaps, race theory. Indeed, reflecting on the absence of a distinctive critical legal feminist 'narrative', Williams suggests that post-modernism offers itself as the only source for an identifiably feminist legal voice, because it is the only narrative which triumphs difference and particularity (Williams, 1991). The essence of the post-modern feminist critique is the dismissal of these 'metanarratives' and a determination to concentrate solely on the particular. Gender questions, as Mary Joe Frug stresses, cannot be considered simply as gender questions. They are, at once, questions of politics, economics, art, culture, text and so on. Thus, sex equality laws and any complementary sex equality debate cannot simply concentrate on the nature of law *per se*, or indeed the operation of those laws in a predetermined political setting. To pursue such a debate is to concede to its preordained and objectified limits. In other words, the sex equality debate cannot presume any given meaning of what sex equality law can possibly mean. There is no one definition of sex, or of woman, of equality, or of law (Frug, 1992, chs. 2, 7–8).

Undoubtedly the most substantive account of post-modern legal feminism is Drucilla Cornell's. Cornell concentrates on developing a post-modern 'ethics' from the deconstruction of law, which can then furnish a viable feminist political agenda. Founded upon the Derridean deconstruction of 'identities', Cornell seeks to go 'beyond' what she terms the 'premature objectivism' of CLS writers, and most particularly Roberto Unger. More specifically she advocates the capacity of Richard Rorty's 'conversationalism' to effect a fluid theory of communicative or dialogic ethics, as an 'ethic of citizenship':

> Dialogism involves a commitment to universality: we are all to be recognized as participants in our collective conversation, and we are to hold it out as a possibility that generalizable interests will emerge in the course of that conversation. (Cornell, 1985, p. 378)

Cornell's community is a fractured community constituted by multiple interests, and wherein political power is dispersed in a radically plural and, echoing certain CLS scholarship, participatory democracy. The overarching characteristic of the jurisprudence of such a community is its 'transformative potential'. It is a radically destabilised community, fiercely resistant to any objectification of rights. There are no unarguable goods, sex equality included. The concentration on 'transformative potential' is, of course, resonant of Unger's 'transformative rights', but Cornell seeks to go 'beyond' the perceived objectification immanent in Unger's rights thesis, and instead concentrates on the preservation of a 'fluid' ethics (Cornell, 1988; 1992, pp. 59–60). In her recent work, Cornell has characterised this as the 'philosophy of the limit', and has intensified its radically plural ethical component:

> I . . . suggest that the entire project of the philosophy of the limit is driven by an ethical desire to enact the ethical relation. Again, by the ethical relation I mean to indicate the aspiration to a nonviolent relationship to the Other, and to otherness more generally, that assumes responsibility to guard the Other against the appropriation that would deny her difference and singularity. (Cornell, 1992, p. 62)

The preservation of particularity of the individual is thus the key component of the philosophy of the limit.

The effect of this philosophy of the limit on feminist legal theory is considerable, because it denies the phenomenology of such as MacKinnon, which, Cornell suggests, positivises a determination of women and, to use the Heideggerian terminology, women's situation in-the-world (Cornell, 1991, pp. 119–64). There is no fixed female reality. Any feminist 'truth' must be written as feminist 'truths', in the plural. This is an essential analogue of the Derridean conception of justice, as justice in the plural, not the singular, and is the 'responsibility' of feminist legal theory (ibid., pp. 115–16). Rather than the programmes of such as Unger or MacKinnon, the politics of which has served only to objectify, Cornell suggests a 'full program' of transformative rights across society, which will effect a collateral 'equivalence' in the condition of women. Such a programme will inhere in both the ethic of 'respect' and the ethic of 'right':

> We need a full program of rights which will provide women with the conditions for equality of well-being and capability. . . . A program of equivalent rights is the legal expression of the affirmation and valuation of sexual difference. 'Equivalence' means of equal value, but not of equal value because of likeness. Equivalence does not demand that the basis of equality be likeness to men. Such a view would be to deny that we are sexuate beings. Ethical feminism denies the 'truth' of the gender hierarchy by affirming the feminine within sexual difference as other to its current identifications. (Cornell, 1993, pp. 123, 141–2)

The programme of legal and political rights must be part of a far wider reorientation of political and social culture. What Cornell terms the 'dream of a new choreography of sexual difference'

> also has to do with the possibility of democracy itself, once we include participatory, dialogic structures in democracy. The psychical fantasy of Women . . . blocks the dialogue we associate with participatory democracy. Indeed, it blocks the recognition of women as citizens. Therefore it is not enough just to socialize the so-called realm of necessity in order for participatory democracy to exist, although this is clearly an important step in battling against the repudiation of the feminine and the devalorization of feminine virtues. The realm of the political must also be feminized, but in a more radical way than has been suggested. (ibid., pp. 168–9)

To identify 'women' is to deny the particularity of women, and to deny the possibility of emancipation in society. The concentration on the particular situation, as opposed to some metaphysical determination of women in general, clearly subverts any uniform or comprehensive theory of sex equality. Such is the fate of any theory which tries to place such an ephemeral concept as equality at its heart. There is no definition of (sex) equality, or rather there are too many, none of them right as such, and none of them wrong. The philosophy of the limit, the post-modern alternative, is to identify (sex) equality as just one destabilised component in a series of such dialogic encounters, which are themselves constitutive of a radically plural, participatory and community-determined 'ethic of citizenship'.

2 IDENTIFYING THE NEW EUROPEAN WOMAN

What is the philosophy behind sex equality law in the European Community, and more importantly perhaps, what is the philosophy which lies behind the critique of these laws? The first question is perhaps the easier to answer, although the two are very obviously related. The European Community, and its principal jurisprudential organs, most obviously the European Court of Justice, have loudly proclaimed their affiliation with rights and a rights discourse. Not that this was ever the intention of the Treaty-framers, for there is no reference to anything approaching substantive rights in the Rome Treaty (Weiler, 1986, pp. 120–3; Lenaerts, 1991). However, encouraged by the Court, there is now much talk about rights to this and rights to that, and sex equality is very much part of this rights-talk. Once again, this is not the avowed intention of the Community's legislators. There is no express recourse to rights as such in the handful of statutory instruments which are directed towards sex equality. It is, however, explicit in the pervasive Community ideology, and has been more confidently assumed by the Court.

This ideology is, of course, a neoclassical free market one, based primarily on the integrity of the contract. Any rights are predetermined, to some degree, by this ideology. This is why commentators such as Koen Lenaerts can categorise social and aspirational rights, as distinct from fundamental rights (Lenaerts, 1991). Sex equality is a categorised right, defined and determined by the 'limits' of the free market ideology. This is the potential fate of any rights-based theory of law, and the particular fate of a liberal one. Aside from the reality of cultural discrimination in Western Europe, the Community actually enhances sex discrimination by allowing the free market to run and to make its own determination of rights (Fenwick & Hervey, 1995, pp. 443, 449). Thus, as Stuart Holland has recently reminded us, gender discrimination in the Community is deeply structural (Holland, 1993, pp. 156–7). Sonia Mazey has emphasised how the Community labour market actually promotes forms of job segregation which flourish upon gender discrimination (Mazey, 1988, pp. 64–7). Capitalism thrives on inequality. It needs inequality by definition. It needs to exploit, and it seizes upon those disadvantaged or already marginalised. The very ideology of capitalism is discriminatory. Sex discrimination represents the triumph of capitalism; it is a testimony to its success (cf. Fredman, 1992, pp. 30–2). Thus any strategy, based upon 'inequalities' or even upon rights, must be directed against the entire metanarrative of the Community and its ideology.

The fallacy of concentrating on purely legal strategies relating to 'formal' sex equality is plain for all to see. Tinkering around with Article 119, or the handful of equal treatment directives, is not going to make much difference to the situation of the overwhelming number of women in Europe today. Such a strategy is 'limited' for a number of reasons. First, it ignores the vast majority of women who are excluded by the ideology of the right, because they are marginalised from the free market. Women who are outside the workplace are powerless. By way of example, this is particularly apparent in the area of Community social security law. This exclusion is even more rigorous for those women who are outside the family nexus and cannot therefore piggyback on the rights of spouses (Sohrab, 1994, pp. 5–16). Indeed, women inside the family nexus are equally powerless, in that the Community has consistently refused to regulate the family. Housework is not real work in Europe, at least not in jurisprudential terms (Cullen, 1994, pp. 413–17). Yet, as Kirsten Scheiwe has emphasised, the Community and its common market depend upon the integral operation of 'unpaid servicing work', determined by a specious distinction between a private family and a public market (Scheiwe, 1994, pp. 255, 261).

Second, for those who are active participants in the free market, there is the problem that, as a liberal right, any sex equality or equal treatment 'right' is a negative right. This means that the rights are formal, they 'aspire' to an ideal of abstract right and do not address the substantive inequalities which women face in the real Community. A classic example here is Article 5 of the Equal Treatment in Employment directive (76/207), which was supposed to address the problem of harassment in the workplace. As the Rubenstein Report emphasised, it is one thing to write a directive, it is quite another actually to effect a substantive change in the actual situation of women in the workplace. The fate of the Rubenstein Report, and its recommendations regarding harassment, and those subsequently articulated in the Vogel–Polsky Report, are a testimony to the Community's unwillingness to look 'beyond' liberal legalism (Ellis, 1991, pp. 174–8). There is also the related and continuing problem of the consistent recourse, by both legislators and judges, to the male comparator, which is again the result of a determination to approximate to some fictional notion of equality, and bound up with the collateral and perennial problem of sameness and difference. A related example of this cultural malaise is the continued acceptance in EC law of the family unit as the norm, wherein welfare benefits are directed towards the heads of households. The law determines these heads of households as male. A similar example is the fact that any woman dependent upon a man is powerless in EC law unless she can establish herself as a 'spouse' (Scheiwe, 1994, pp. 248–51).

Third, as a related observation, the history of the European Court's interpretation of Article 119 and the equal treatment directives consistently betrays a willingness to determine the principle of equality in the light of the ideology of a free market. Chris Docksey has referred to the Court's apparent reflexive 'deference to economic conditions' (Docksey, 1991, pp. 274–6). In landmark cases, such as *Defrenne*, although the Court was prepared to effect the principle of equal pay, it was clear that it did so primarily because such a principle was in line with the wider ambitions of a liberal free market (*Defrenne*). As one commentator has noted, Article 119 is no more than a 'by-product' of market regulation (Scheiwe, 1994, p. 245). As Philippa Watson has recently suggested, the case law makes it quite clear that the 'principle' of sex equality is a 'variable' one, subject to the wider ambitions of the Community's political economy (Watson, 1995). A notorious example here is the

Court's ruling in *Bilka-Kaufhaus,* which permitted indirect discrimination if it could be 'objectively justified', which, of course, meant economically justified (*Bilka-Kaufhaus*). It is all too clear that the social ideal of sex equality has never alone been sufficient for either the politicians or the judges of the new Europe (Meehan, 1990, p. 185). Any form of social justice is rationalised as desirable only because it will make the market more productive. It is regrettable that this rationale remains at the heart of even the most radical of contemporary programmes for social reform in the Community (Holland, 1993, pp. 157–9).

What is perhaps most instructive is the fact that the new Europe clearly intends to do little or nothing about sex equality. Sure, it may tinker a little more with Article 119 and even throw in a few more equal treatment directives. But it will certainly not look to address the substantive problems which lie behind a liberal rights thesis based on the fiction of abstract equality. This is all too apparent from the Maastricht Treaty. The principle of subsidiarity actually militates against any uniform approach to the problem of sex discrimination in the workplace (Cullen, 1994, pp. 408–9). This is not a problem *per se,* but it is within the particular context of a liberal rights-based ideology, with its concomitant pretence to universality. Similarly, Article 6 of the Social Policy Agreement repeats a commitment to equal pay, but in doing so merely reaffirms a commitment to formal equality alone (Scheiwe, 1994, p. 244).

Perhaps even more unfortunate is the reluctance of sex equality commentators to perceive the limitations, not merely of Community sex equality law, but of the European Community as a whole. It is the very ideology of the Community which must be reformed, not merely the text of its sex equality laws or judgments. There is much talk about the need to effect substantive, as opposed to merely formal, equality. There is certainly no doubting the inadequacy of formal equality, but how will substantive equality be effected, never mind defined? Feminist critiques of Community sex equality law still cling to an illusion of equality. Thus Evelyn Ellis rightly condemns an idea of formal equality which encourages women to 'strive for male patterns of work and to conform to existing male values'. But, in its place, she wants 'genuine equality' to be effected by a wider legal and political strategy (Ellis, 1991, pp. 206–8). I would not disagree with the need for a wider strategy, providing it is one which is at once aware of the reality of particular situations, and the desirability of defining woman in the particular. But is there really a need to try to define a vision of genuine equality? Whose definition is this going to be? Any such definition can only assume some constituent definitions, not just of equality, but of women.

A more promising critic is Gillian More, who acknowledges that:

> The Community's formula for sex equality is . . . abstract, narrow and rigid: it is conceptually incapable of eradicating all but the most superficial inequalities faced by women. It helps only those women workers who are already well assimilated to men; it reinforces inequalities based on gender differences; it restricts the use of positive action; and it masks the fact that many of women's inequalities at work are intimately related to their role in the family. (More, 1993, p. 64)

More recognises that 'equality', aside from being a rather ephemeral concept, is one which is all too easily determined in relation to dominant male comparators. Following MacKinnon's thesis, More rejects 'equality' and the related notion of sameness and difference, and instead supports the idea of 'disadvantage' as a guiding concept by which to adjudge alleged gender discrimination. The overriding quality of such an approach, as she acknowledges, is that it does not assume any metanarrative of the female condition in the EC, but rather concentrates on the particular situation of each disadvantaged woman (ibid., pp. 65–74).

3 SOME CONCLUSIONS

It is here that a post-modern feminist approach can offer a means of going 'beyond' sex equality. Most immediately, rather than attempting to define equality and then concentrate strategies around this definition in relation to some sort of determined right, post-modern feminism demands that the position of women in law and in society must be addressed from outside the 'limits' of the law. In other words, there must be a wider critique of society and culture, with the legal critique as merely a constituent part. There is evidence that feminist critiques of Community sex equality law are moving in this direction (Fenwick & Hervey, 1995, pp. 470–1). Louise Ackers has recently emphasised that too much reliance on the law actually serves to distract attention from patent political inadequacies (Ackers, 1994, p. 392). Sandra Fredman has similarly appealed for 'legal strategies' to be accompanied by a 'much more radical focus on structural disadvantage and the causes thereof' (Fredman, 1992, p. 134). Sonia Mazey has stressed the need to address the deeper structural problems of gender inequality. Only a concerted political initiative can attack the residual strength of both direct and indirect discrimination, and hope to make a real impact. Law and legal initiatives, she suggests, have 'to date made no discernible impact on the problem of sex discrimination in the labour market' (Mazey, 1988, pp. 63, 70, 82). As Rhode emphasises, classical liberalism is an ideology geared to the exploitation of the marginalised and disempowered. The European Community aspires to be the apogee of a classical liberal 'state', founded upon a free and common market. A post-modern feminist critique of sex discrimination in the Community must identify precisely what it is writing against and appreciate the strength of its ideological oppressor. The problem with the jurisprudentially determined 'economic women' in the Community is not with the determination of woman, but with the determination of 'economic'. This is the deconstructive role for post-modern feminism.

The reconstructive role is just as important. Tantalisingly, it is here that the new post-Maastricht Europe might have something to offer. There are two particular ideas which we have already identified as central to post-modern feminist legal thinking, both of which have recently been redefined by the new Europe. The first of these is citizenship, and the second is democracy. As I suggested in chapter 5, these two concepts are virtually coexistent in the debate surrounding the possible radical rewriting of European political thought. Rhode, Majury and Cornell all suggest that there must be an alternative idea of citizenship as social citizenship. At the same time, by redefining a social citizenship it is possible to redefine rights as social, as opposed to liberal individual rights. Of course, as we have already seen, the much triumphed conception of rights in the Maastricht Treaty is a decidedly political conception, where, most notoriously, citizenship of the Union is still to be determined via citizenship of a nation-state. The exclusionary nature of such a definition, and particularly its role in constructing the effective exclusion of women, has already been noted by a number of commentators. The only justiciable 'rights' which flow from Article 8 citizenship are those pertaining to the Community laws of free movement and related legislation. As Louise Ackers has thus concluded, Article 8 citizenship does more to condemn women to an inferior constitutional status than emancipate them from an already real status of economic inferiority. Only a conception of social citizenship, in which legal and welfare protection is extended to all persons, regardless of their role in the market, can hope to address the abuses of gender discrimination (Ackers, 1994).

However, despite these immediately discouraging prognoses, critics such as Paul Close, as we noted in chapter 5, have already detected a movement in Community rhetoric towards what he defines as a 'new social citizenship'. Social citizenship is the logical supplement to any socially, as opposed to purely economically, determined Union. It might, he predicts, be the determination favoured by any Union which evolves along these lines (Close, 1995, pp. 45–81, 198–222). Such a conception is a post-modern one, simply because it is a post-political one, and the modern has always defined itself as the political. The emphasis on conversationalism and the dialogic 'ethic of citizenship', as presented by Cornell, thus becomes a very real and viable model for an evolving Union conception of citizenship. Such a communicatively constructed citizenship will be effected only through the re-empowerment of marginalised, or 'silenced', voices, of which women are just one. In other word, there must be a radical transformation in the forms of governance in the new Europe. As Close emphasises, the reality of social citizenship in the new Europe is conditional upon such a transformation. Power must be pluralised, fragmented between various interests, individual and corporate (Close, 1995, pp. 242–68).

This introduces the second and related idea central to post-modern feminist thinking, that of alternative conceptions of democracy. Once again, the new Europe has gestured in this direction, in deciding to be more democratic, or at least appearing to be more democratic. Unfortunately, as we have seen, it assumes that the most immediate form of democracy is representative democracy. There are alternatives. Most obviously, there is the idea of pluralism and participatory democracy, as espoused by countless CLS writers in various forms, and taken on by a number of the more critical feminist legal theorists. As we have already noted, for such as Rhode or Cornell, the fragmentation of power in a more plural polity, along with the enhanced potential to exercise power in a participatory democracy, are central tenets of an alternative post-modern feminist political agenda. Only this fragmentation will give women the voice by which to 'write' the feminine in a participatory democracy. At first glance, the new Europe, like the old one, held in the thrall of the nation-states, might not seem to enjoy a particularly fertile potential. This suspicion is enhanced, as we have already seen, by the pervasive assumption that democracy can only really mean representative democracy.

However, the tantalising exception, as ever, is the much maligned concept of subsidiarity. The obfuscation surrounding the precise meaning of subsidiarity, as we know, is already the stuff of legend. Subsidiarity had to mean everything and anything to everybody and anybody. There is a 'fatal confusion' with regard to the extent to which the operation of subsidiarity will centralise or decentralise power. If the principle only enjoys meaning within a recognisably centralised federal state, then subsidiarity will not be a principle which helps the empowerment of any disempowered voices. Neither will the decentralisation of power back to the nation-states, the interpretation loudly articulated by such as John Major, do more to help. However, a radical interpretation of subsidiarity, stripping power away from both Brussels and Westminster, could do much to empower both interests and individuals, and not only on a classically functional-pluralist basis. More recently, as we have seen, David Coombes and Ian Harden have suggested that subsidiarity encapsulates the spirit of a plural, participatory democracy (Coombes, 1994, pp. 157–78; Harden, 1994, pp. 613, 620, 624). Subsidiarity can provide the radically destabilised, plural and participatory model of governance which post-modern feminism advocates as the only viable means by which women can gain a 'voice' in society, and thus contribute to the constitution of 'ethical citizenship'. It may not be as whimsical as at first glance it seems to be. It can certainly be argued that it is likely to benefit women in concrete individual situations more effectively than the continual, and flawed, attempts to reach an understanding about what a jurisprudence of equality might mean. As a concluding, and related, point, the feminist voice in European studies is not silenced. In fact it is a louder voice than that of many marginalised interests in the new Europe. There is therefore a responsibility incumbent upon the feminist voice in Europe, and that is to speak for all the many marginalised and disempowered interests. The white, working, middle-class European woman is still in an infinitely more empowered position than the black, migrant, unemployed male. Feminism, and particularly post-modern feminism, should have the confidence to present itself as a flagship for the many 'silenced' in a Europe, the political and economic ideology of which is founded upon the exploitation of the weak and the economically impoverished.

8 Human Rights in the New European Union

The European Community, and now the European Union, has increasingly talked about rights, and more and more about human or fundamental rights. The more it has talked about these rights, the louder has been the surrounding criticism of its efforts. Most recently, it has been repeatedly suggested that the new Europe is not taking rights 'seriously' (Coppel & O'Neill, 1992). In this chapter, I want first to discuss the state of human rights in European law and to assess the veracity of these critiques. In the second section I then want to suggest some alternative approaches to human rights which might be more appropriate and perhaps more workable in the new Europe.

1 HUMAN RIGHTS IN TODAY'S EUROPE

There is no human rights basis to the Treaty framework, and it is this omission that lies at the root of any perceived inadequacies. The ambition of the Community has always remained firmly economic (cf. Frowein et al., 1986, pp. 231–4). The Rome Treaty was very much a product of its time and, despite some flowery rhetoric, human rights was never part of what Weiler terms the founding fathers' 'conception' (Weiler, 1986, pp. 110–13). Since the first days of the Community, the nation-states have proved to be especially intransigent when it has come to renouncing their so-called 'margin of appreciation' in the area of human rights (Clapham, 1990, p. 311). This fact has led to two immediate conclusions. First, in the absence of any definitional guide, there is a considerable amount of confusion with regard to what a human right in the Community is. All sorts of things are bandied around as potential fundamental or human rights. Some commentators have suggested that administrative law rights, such as rights to a fair hearing, are fundamental human rights (Schwarze, 1986). Numerous areas of social law, such as the much vaunted social dialogue, are frequently portrayed as human rights. Indeed, even the free movement rights are often presented as human rights. Thus the European Court's refusal to support the application of the Spanish fishermen to fish in certain waters was alleged to be a breach of their 'human rights' (Churchill & Foster, 1987, pp. 430–3).

Clearly, there needs to be some form of definitional realignment, otherwise the demarcation of fishing rights will be jurisprudentially indistinguishable in human rights terms from the worst forms of cruel and unusual punishment. The most popular distinction is made between 'fundamental' and merely 'aspirational' rights. In an influential essay, Koen Lenaerts has developed this distinction into a 'concentric circles' model for a 'catalogue' of fundamental rights protected in European law. There are four of these circles; first, those contained in the European Convention, second, those 'general principles of law' as articulated by the European Court on the basis of Article 164, third, those fundamental rights attached to Community citizenship, and fourth, those that are 'aspirational', into which are bundled social and economic rights (Lenaerts, 1991). Though certainly viable, I shall suggest in the second part of this chapter that such a demarcation remains firmly within an essentially modernist liberal philosophy of rights, and thus similarly trapped by all the tensions which such a discourse cannot resolve.

The second result of the absence of a human rights basis in the Treaty framework is that the evolution of a human rights jurisprudence is almost exclusively the work of the European Court. Although initially wary of overt promotion of human rights, the establishment of core constitutional principles, namely supremacy and direct effect, provided the impetus for the Court. Famously in 1969, in the *Stauder* case, it articulated a determination to protect 'the fundamental human rights enshrined in the general principles of Community law' (*Stauder*). The following year, in *Internationale Handelsgesellschaft*, the Court implicitly approved the Advocate-General's suggestion that such a jurisprudence was to be found in the 'philosophical, political and legal substratum common to the Member-States' (*Internationale Handeslgesellschaft*). The idea of constructing a human rights jurisprudence from member state provisions smacked of minimalism (cf. Rasmussen, 1986, p. 399). It has been commonly suggested that the 1970s, and particularly the *Nold no. 2* and *Hauer* cases, bore testimony to a more confident and aggressive Court (Dallen, 1990, p. 781; Bibas, 1992, pp. 254–7). But, in terms of judicial methodology at least, this is not really the case. In *Nold no. 2*, the Court continued its essentially comparativist approach. Moreover, at the same time, it reinforced a crucial concession to the basic economic imperatives of the Community legal order, by conceding that a compromise had to be made between the 'substance' of fundamental human rights and 'certain limits justified by the overall objectives pursued by the Community' (*Nold no. 2*).

The *Hauer* case was perhaps more revealing in that the Court emphasised the inclusion of the European Convention as a potential source for human rights, as a supplement to those to be found in member state constitutions (*Hauer*). In the absence of anything more inspirational, recourse to the Convention has proved to be increasingly popular. Lenaerts has suggested that whilst Community law provides a human rights jurisprudence at a Community level, the Convention provides such a jurisprudence at nation-state level (Lenaerts, 1991, pp. 371–2). If this is so, it does not therefore widen the definition of Community human rights at all. Moreover, it is subject to the pervasive concern with regard to the status of the Convention in Community law. This status is dubious simply because the precise relation between Community and national legal systems remains uncertain. In the present quasi-federal order, because national law seems to remain supreme in certain areas, application of the Convention is not universal amongst the member states. Until we reach a stage where each nation-state is required to incorporate the Convention into national law, then we shall remain short of a comprehensive legal resource, and citizens of one nation-state will be better protected than citizens of another. Citizens of the UK, of course, are least well protected of all. The record of the UK before the European Court of Human Rights is notoriously shabby, and not surprisingly the call for incorporation of the Convention either in Community law or directly into national law has been strongest amongst UK commentators (Bingham,

1993; Warbick, 1994, pp. 43–6). However, as the recent decision in *Brind* has demonstrated, the UK courts remain strenuously opposed to any incorporation 'through the back door' (*Brind*). As yet, therefore, recourse to the Convention cannot be used as a viable alternative to a comprehensive articulation of a Community human rights jurisprudence in the form of a catalogue, or such like.

The activism of the European Court thus remains the only genuinely dynamic source for a human rights jurisprudence. One of the most thoughtful commentators on this activism is Joseph Weiler. Weiler suggests that the development of a human rights jurisprudence is entirely the product of the Court's activism:

> The Court has been content to leave the precise legal basis vague and it is more honest to recognize the new jurisprudence for what it is: a judicial leap rooted more in the political philosophy of the Community and its Member States than in strict legal grounds. (Weiler, 1986, p. 1118)

According to Weiler, the *Hauer* case is crucial in signalling a second, more aggressive, stage in the development of this jurisprudence, in that the Court claimed sole jurisdictional authority for human rights issues in Community law (ibid., pp. 1121–34). Yet, despite applauding this aggression, Weiler joins a chorus of commentators urging both judges and politicians to make a more definitive statement. For Weiler, it is a matter of fundamental credibility:

> What is at stake then, is not the fear of excessive zeal in asserting individual rights but fear of the opposite: a reluctance of the Court to exercise a sufficiently robust individual protection policy. If there is distrust it is not a distrust of a Court overreaching itself in protecting the individual, but of a Court not reaching far enough. (ibid., p. 1109; cf. Dallen, 1990, p. 762)

Implicit in any such argument is applause for the diminution of nation-state authority in human rights matters. Moreover, the next step, as Weiler rightly suggests, is for the Court to determine that a Community human rights jurisprudence applies across both Community and member state jurisdictions. It is the inevitable logic of integration. To a certain extent, this might be detected in the early *Rutili* decision, where the Court confirmed that member states were 'in principle, free to determine the requirement of public policy in the light of their national needs' but that this determination was 'subject' to Community control (*Rutili*). Subsequent case law has painted a rather inconsistent picture. Although the decision in *Cinéthèque* leant in the direction suggested in *Rutili*, in *Klensch* the Court seemed to be only too keen to stress the limitations of its own jurisdiction to Community matters only (*Cinéthèque*; *Klensch*). More recently still, in *Bostock*, the Court has again reaffirmed its subservience to national court jurisdiction as a matter of policy (*Bostock*; cf. Weiler & Lockhart, 1995, pp. 605–18). In *Demirel*, the Court further articulated its commitment to a clear demarcation of interests between human rights pertaining to Community law and the residual 'margin of appreciation' pertaining to national courts (*Demirel*). It was a sharp reminder of the politics of Community human rights. More recently again, in *Wachauf*, whilst giving rein to the rhetoric of human rights, the Court was careful to emphasise that any fundamental rights were not in fact 'absolute', but rather subject to the wider economic and social ambitions of the Community (*Wachauf*). This second wave of human rights decisions has thus not been entirely convincing. The preparedness of certain member state courts to dismiss the substance of Community human rights provisions is perhaps instructive. In *Fragd*, for example, the Italian constitutional court was prepared to breach the basic principle of Community law supremacy rather than submit to what it perceived to be inadequate Community human rights law (cf. Schermers, 1990).

Post-Maastricht, the Community is no nearer being founded upon a firm human rights basis than it was before. Although there is, as ever, much talk in all the institutions about the European rights discourse, there is precious little in the Treaty that is tangible or even useful for the new European citizen. Indeed, the determination of the citizen as a kind of superior, and better protected, individual in the Community is itself problematic (Closa, 1994). In the matter of determining citizenship, the member states remain all-powerful, and the fate of human rights lies at the whim of the national interest. This is perhaps the most disappointing of the many disappointing aspects of the Maastricht Treaty. Writing in 1990, Andrew Clapham emphasised that any refined concept of Community citizenship could only have meaning if it was backed up by a Community catalogue of human rights in tandem with a constitutional commitment to the Convention. The key characteristic of such a constitutional commitment being a determination to cut through the jurisdictional niceties which continue to hamstring the Community's attempts to broker a human rights jurisprudence (Clapham, 1990, pp. 356–66). Read in this light the failings of Maastricht become ever more glaring. Patrick Twomey has rightly affirmed that 'the TEU's failure to deal adequately with human rights issues represents a lost opportunity and a fundamental defect in a Community in the process of expanding towards the Urals' (Twomey, 1994, p. 121). In 1989, in anticipation of Maastricht, Jacques Delors said that the primary responsibility of the politicians was now one of putting 'some flesh on the Community's bones' and giving it a 'little soul' (Clapham, 1990, p. 366). The need is clearly as pressing now, in 1996, as it was in 1989.

2 DEFINING THE EUROPEAN HUMAN RIGHT

The absence of some sort of human rights charter is regrettable, as indeed is the absence of any form of definitive Community statement on human rights. However, I would suggest that the real problems run deeper still and ultimately lie in the philosophy of right which the Community espouses. That philosophy is quite clearly a liberal rights philosophy, and like any such philosophy revolves around the two fundamental concepts of freedom and equality. These two concepts have become synonymous with the modernist vision of politics, as established in the eighteenth and nineteenth centuries by Rousseau, Kant, Hegel and a host of other political philosophers of similar persuasion. The modernist conception of human rights is thus founded on these twin concepts. Although freedom and equality might seem to be unarguable 'rights', the difficulties are encountered when these rights are translated into the political situation, because all too often there appear to be conflicting rights; the right of free speech vs. the right to privacy is just one example. Any legal order encounters these difficulties, but the Community legal order seems to experience them more intensely than most. It does so because it is a political and legal ideology specifically constructed from a particular modern classical liberal political and economic ideology. It thus offers itself as a prime example of how tortuous it is to try to construct a fundamental human rights jurisprudence from such an ideology. As I mentioned earlier, in the absence of any abstract human rights conception in the Community, commentators have tended to look at what have been termed 'aspirational' rights. These are generally economic and social rights which pertain to the economic and social legal system which founds the Community. These are the politically situated rights which commentators have taken to be the fundamental human rights of the Community. These are, as I have already indicated, the fundamental human rights presented by the European Court. Freedom and equality are taken as the philosophical concepts of modern rights discourse, and translated into the liberal political ideology of the Community and its common market.

Freedom lies at the very heart of Community law. It is commonly said to be founded upon four core freedoms of movement: of persons, of goods, of services and of capital. Quite obviously, these are essentially economic rights, and it is a freedom which relates purely to effecting a single common market. The extent to which various 'freedoms' conflict in Community economic law are notorious. The attempt to regulate the so-called 'free' market in the field of competition law is itself an acknowledgement of the impossibility of 'pure' competition. The alternative, what has become known as 'workable' competition, requires the amelioration of the so-called 'freedoms' of movement. According to Loukas Tsoukalis, no 'political economy', of which the Community is a prime example, can ever give full rein to any economic freedom. In the particular context of the Community, these freedoms are always subject to the constraining demands of the nation-states (Tsoukalis, 1991, chs. 2–3). As Francis Snyder has emphasised, given the inherently contradictory demands of a legally enforced free-market ideology, the uncertainties and inconsistencies of the European Court are hardly surprising (Snyder, 1990, pp. 63–99).

As we have already seen in the previous chapter, an alternative and perhaps more revealing example of this tension lies in sex equality law. The demands of sex 'equality' play directly against the idea of a wholly 'free' market. A free market, effected essentially by an idea of competition, seeks to exploit. Such is the rationale of competition. Yet any form of competition or exploitation is going to promote disequilibrium. Gender discrimination in the market place is a prime example of systematic disequilibrium. The Community labour market actually promotes forms of job segregation which flourish upon gender discrimination (Mazey, 1988, pp. 64–7). The Community strategy of restricting the 'free' market by means of certain 'equal' treatment directives is inherently flawed. First, because it leaves out those women whom it deems to be outside what it defines as the workplace (Cullen, 1994, pp. 413–17). Second, because a system of formal rights of equality fails to address substantive inequalities, such as sexual harassment (Ellis, 1991, pp. 174–8). Third, because when push comes to shove, the Court has consistently revealed itself prepared to compromise its idea of equality in order to facilitate its definition of economic freedom (Docksey, 1991, pp. 274–6). Political or jurisprudential 'equality' is too ephemeral a concept itself to redress the substantive inequalities which women endure in the Community (More, 1993).

A final, and popularly cited, example of the tensions that exist in the Community determination of these freedoms lies in the critique of Irish abortion cases. Here the Court's understanding of human rights was indirectly challenged by a series of cases which seemed to establish a potential conflict between the right of free movement of services and the morality integral to the legal code of a member state. In the *Grogan* case, the question revolved around the legality or otherwise of the distribution of leaflets giving advice on abortion which was alleged to be contrary to national law and Article 40.3.3 of the Irish Constitution. The Irish supreme court approved an Article 177 reference to the European Court on the grounds that operation of the national law might represent a potential infringement of Article 60 of the EC Treaty, the free movement of services. The European Court upheld the free movement right over the Irish law, which a number of commentators have suggested was more 'fundamental' than the merely 'aspirational' right of Article 60 (*Grogan*). The perceived championing of an economic right over a moral one has led to much critical commentary. According to Diarmuid Rossa Phelan:

> The direction of the ECJ's jurisprudence dealing with the effects of fundamental rights appears from the *Grogan* case to be subject to an internal independent rationale and momentum towards objectives drawn from essentially economic Treaties between national governments . . . . *SPUC v Grogan* was the product of a contingent mode of legal thought which, if unchecked, will shape both the normative structure and the substance of fundamental rights in the European Union. (Phelan, 1992, p. 689)

Gráinne de Burca has gone further, and to the heart of the matter, by suggesting that the Court's reluctance to embrace a fundamental human rights position in deciding the case reveals a deeper problem endemic to its role in ameliorating member state political and jurisdictional sensitivities. It will, she concludes, 'undermine any belief in the Court as a principled and consistent adjudicator with a developed vision of its role in the Community legal order.' Echoing some of the earlier observations with regard to the inconsistencies which have resulted from a human rights jurisprudence created essentially on the hoof by the Court, she further concludes that,

> the incremental and gradualist expansion of protection for these 'general principles' within Community law has resulted in a haphazard and unpredictable approach which can hardly be more palatable to those states opposing incorporation than would formal accession by the Community to the Convention. (de Burca, 1993, pp. 317–8)

'Freedom' is not then an absolute. It is not determinate. One commentator has even gone so far as to say that the understanding of 'freedom' as articulated by the Community and its legal system is more of a threat to human rights than a guarantor of them (Clapham, 1990, p. 329). In the light of these seeming indeterminacies and inconsistencies, two of the most strident critics, Coppel and O'Neill, have suggested that,

> it must be questioned whether the court has ever been motivated by a concern for any supposed lack of adequate protection of fundamental rights within the European Community . . . the court has employed fundamental rights instrumentally, so as to accelerate the process of legal integration in the Community. It has not protected these fundamental rights for their own sake. It has not taken these rights seriously. (Coppel & O'Neill, 1992, pp. 227–8)

Emphasising the ulterior imperialistic motives of the Court, they conclude that the 'high rhetoric of human rights protection can be seen as no more than a vehicle for the court to extend the scope and impact of European law' (ibid., p. 245). This is an ambitious critique and has itself attracted some similarly strident counter-critiques. Weiler and Lockhart have challenged the imputation that the Court has all along been acting out of deceit, with an enduring ulterior motive. However, their suggestion that the Court has only been able to develop a jurisprudence from the legislation and ideology made available to it does not of itself entirely dispel the validity of Coppel and O'Neill's argument (Weiler & Lockhart, 1995). If anything, it legitimates it. It may not be the Court's fault, but the fact remains that the Community idea of human rights, to the extent that it has one, founded upon politicised determinations of freedom and equality, is simply not enough. They are quite right in confirming that it is naive to believe that any human rights discourse can be founded upon an 'absolute' determination of rights. But this should surely suggest, not that we stumble on making up definitions as we go along, but that we look to a radically alternative understanding of what human rights might be made to mean.

3 TOWARDS A POSTMODERN CONCEPTION OF HUMAN RIGHTS

Is there an alternative to the pervasive liberal modernist rights-based approach to human rights? I would suggest that there is, and that an alternative distinctively post-modern conception of human rights might be better suited to the kind of post-modern European polity which is beginning to emerge. The idea of a post-modern human rights became a central theme in a series of lectures organised under the auspices of the Oxford Amnesty Lectures of 1993, and I want to concentrate on three of these lectures in particular; those of Jean-François Lyotard, Richard Rorty and John Rawls.

The name of Jean-François Lyotard is one of the most readily associated with post-modernism. According to Lyotard, post-modernism 'reflects' upon and 'respects' the particular, as opposed to the dehumanising and 'totalising' potential of modernism and its 'metanarratives'. Indeed, he suggests that post-modernism, in this sense, is all about justice. The ambition of post-modernism is to reintroduce the excluded into the political dialogue (Lyotard, 1984b; Lyotard, 1988). In his 1993 lecture, 'The Other's Rights', Lyotard develops these themes in the particular area of human rights. In fact, what Lyotard impresses is the fact that human rights are beyond the liberal conception of rights, because they apply to those who are excluded from ordinary legal rights. This enjoys a particular resonance with regard to those who are excluded from the European legal order, such as migrants and non-economic actors; the situation of whom we have already noted. The 'foreclosure of the Other' characterises the 'post-modern affliction' itself. The most fundamental human right of all, according to Lyotard, is the right to articulate and to reciprocate. It is a right to 'respect'. In other words, it is the right to engage in dialogue. Implicitly, this means, most importantly of all, the right to engage in justice, in jurisprudential dialogue. These, he suggests, are the 'characteristics of justice itself':

> Let us take it that the capacity to speak to others is a human right, and perhaps the most fundamental of right. If the use of his capacity is forbidden, whether de facto, by

> some injustice of fate, or on principle, for example as a punishment, a harm is inflicted on the speaker thus constrained. He is set apart from the speech community of interlocutors. To no one is he any longer someone other, nor is anyone now his other. (Lyotard, 1993b, pp. 140–1)

To deny articulation is to deny particularity and identity. It is here, in such a post-modern definition of human rights, that dialogic participation can be seen to be an essential component.

In his lecture, 'Human Rights, Rationality, and Sentimentality', Richard Rorty, like Lyotard, is concerned with the potential of liberal human rights to exclude. In Rorty's opinion those excluded, the 'others', are those who are not perceived as conforming to certain norms, derived from a spurious rationalism. Rorty's own brand of neo-pragmatism is, of course, famously founded on a rejection of the imperialistic qualities of modernism and Enlightenment rationalism. His politics, like Lyotard's, is geared to facilitating conversation between the included and the excluded (Rorty, 1980; 1989). His idea of a human rights, therefore, is of a human rights without rationalist or metaphysical foundations. It is not, then, the familiar human rights of universal morality. There is no presumption of universalism, but rather a concern with self-consciousness (Rorty, 1993, pp. 112–18). A post-modern human rights is about activating and perhaps challenging moral feelings, not moral knowledge. It is about reintroducing 'niceness' in place of any supposed 'obedience to the moral law':

> We pragmatists argue from the fact that the emergence of the human rights culture seems to owe nothing to increased moral knowledge, and everything to hearing sad and sentimental stories . . . . We go on to argue: Since no useful work seems to be done by insisting on a purportedly ahistorical human nature, there probably is no such nature, or at least nothing in that nature that is relevant to our moral choices. (ibid., pp. 118–19, 130)

The 'manipulation of sentiment' will realize far more for the cause of human rights, than endless rationalisation about morality, duty and obligation (ibid., pp. 120–1).

It is, then, a matter of redefining what is meant, not only by 'rights', but by 'human'. People should be 'respected' as people, not as rational human beings. We do not need to find things in common to define the human being. Respect does not presume commonality. If there is no commonality, then there cannot be an identifiable body of excluded. Instead, there is particularity, in which everyone is other, and no one is. Ultimately, the essence of a post-modern human rights is the 'manipulation of sentiment'. Using the example of gang rape, as witnessed in the former Yugoslavia, Rorty suggests that the sentimental response was both more valid and more important than any question of the supposed rationality or non-rationality of the act. We do not need to know that gang rape is against the moral law to know that it is repulsive and cruel. A post-modern human rights can be founded, not on rightness, but on 'niceness' and on a sentimental 'respect'. It is reason enough to respect another person (Rorty, 1993, pp. 122, 125–7, 133–4). The last two centuries, he concludes, progressing from modern Europe to post-modern Europe,

> are most easily understood not as a period of deepening understanding of the nature of rationality or of morality, but rather as one in which there occurred an astonishingly rapid progress of sentiments, in which it has become much easier for us to be moved to action by sad and sentimental stories. (ibid., p. 134)

John Rawls is not a name that is as readily associated with post-modernism. Yet his recent work, culminating most obviously in his recent *Political Liberalism*, reveals the full extent to which Rawls has moved away from his earlier Kantianism in such as *A Theory of Justice* (Rawls, 1973; 1993a). There are three fundamental principles in this non-foundational political, as opposed to philosophical, liberalism: pluralism, reasonableness, as intersubjectively and conversationally determined, and constructivism. These principles lead to an 'idea of a political conception of justice as a freestanding view starting from the fundamental ideas of a democratic society and presupposing no particular wider doctrine' (Rawls, 1993a, p. 40). The morality which characterises such a society is thus a plural and constructivist morality. It is not fundamental in any other way. It accommodates consensus and respect, and is dialogically constructed with these twin ambitions in mind (ibid., pp. 164–72). Such a political liberalism is of the same vintage as Rorty's self-styled post-modern bourgeois liberalism (Ward, 1995).

Rawls' essay 'The Law of Peoples' serves to reinforce this impression. At the very outset of his lecture, Rawls emphasises that a human rights thesis is a political, not a philosophical, exercise. Because political justice is not universal, and not about universalism, then human rights, likewise, is not universal, or about universalism. Such is the critical error of received contemporary modernist approaches to the question of human rights. A theory of human rights must, instead, be dialogically constructed from the 'distinct structure' of the particular 'social framework'. This, he perceptively adds, is a human rights appropriate to the post-modern world of international law and politics, a world in which our understanding of politics is no longer geared to the idea of sovereignty and of nation-states (Rawls, 1993b, pp. 42–9). Human rights, properly understood, can only be defined as themselves contributing to the constraint of the nation-state. Human rights can, thus, be identified with post-modernism. They characterise a world beyond sovereignty (ibid., pp. 68–71). This, of course, has a particular resonance in European legal studies, where so much is now talked about a theory of constitutions and politics which is 'beyond sovereignty'. He concludes, in words which strikingly echo Rorty's essay, that the 'law of peoples' must be 'based on a public political conception of justice and not on a comprehensive religious, philosophical, or moral doctrine' (ibid., p. 82).

A post-modern human rights is, then, a human rights which respects the particular, rather than idolises the universal. It is not a human rights which seeks to justify itself by appeals to the concepts such as absolute freedom or absolute equality. It does not perceive itself to have failed if it cannot achieve such absolute ideals, or even define them. It is not defeated by the mere fact that the political rights which are devolved from such metaphysical concepts are seen to conflict. Post-modern human rights only exist in the concrete political situation. Their jurisprudential coherence in the abstract is not an issue of importance. To use Rorty's terminology, they are about sentimentality, rather than reason, feelings rather than coherence. It is enough to feel that something is wrong, or to use Rawls' favoured term, unfair. It does not need to be rationalised as being against some sort of fundamental right.

This, I would suggest, is a model which can complement the politics of the new post-modern Europe. It does not depend for its existence on the resolution of apparently irreconcilable tensions between the various so-called 'fundamental' and 'aspirational' rights. It does not depend on the determination of Union citizenship or participation of the individual as an economic actor. A post-modern human rights is not hamstrung simply because of conflicting rights, such as the rights to free movement of services and to life, as in the Irish abortion cases. Rather it concerns itself with what is 'fair' in the light of the pervasive political morality of the community. It is not preoccupied with questions of what is or is not philosophically 'right'. Such questions are as capable of resolution by feelings as by reason. Similarly, in a post-modern human rights, a woman is determined as an individual, not as a woman. Her political situation is not dependent upon a determination of equality in the context of a particular understanding of Community freedom. It is simply a matter of fairness and respect, not of equality or participation as a rational economic actor.

A post-modern human rights 'respects', rather than determines, the individual. Most importantly it does not then determine the non-individual, the excluded other. To use Rorty's conceptualisation, it means that everybody is other in a political situation of immanent reciprocity, and nobody is only other. Human rights properly understood is not in the gift of the nation-states or of the new Union, and it is certainly not something which can be determined by reference to any spurious political determination of citizenship. We are all participants in the human rights dialogue, and human rights are ours to determine, to judge and to feel. Human rights, in the final analysis, do not need the justification of European Union approval. They are immanent to the individual *qua* individual. They do not need to be validated in any charter of so-called fundamental freedoms, and they do not only exist when presented in such a charter or created by a supposedly activist legal tribunal. Such a charter and such a tribunal can only acknowledge the importance of such rights to a given community. It cannot create them, for they already are, created by our own sentiments and feelings, and determinative of, and determined by, our own existence in conversationally constructive communities.

Part IV

Reprise and Envoi

9 Europe and Beyond

The purpose of this final chapter is to suggest that the European Union can be best understood as a post-modern polity, and perhaps, as a post-modern text. Indeed, this has been the ultimate ambition of all the chapters which make up this book. From a textual perspective, the European Union is beset by problems of identity, and so, too, are European legal studies. From a political and constitutional perspective, the European Union continues to defy objective determination. It does not fit comfortably with the familiar modernist theories of law and society. The fit that it presently enjoys is as unconvincing as it is uncomfortable. In the first section of this final chapter I want to discuss further the pervasive questions of identity which the new Europe has thrown up. In the second and third sections, I then want to rewrite a distinctively post-modern identity for the new European Union. In doing so, I want to emphasise the extent to which such a rewriting can effect a Europe 'beyond' that which is presently described, and which can better realise the aspirations of a twenty-first century, and distinctly post-modern, society.

1 QUESTIONS OF IDENTITY

As I suggested in the very first chapter, the pervasive problems in today's Europe are problems of identity. Moreover, the problem of identity is inextricably linked to the question of legitimacy. The legitimacy of the new Europe depends upon the resolution of its identity (Garcia, 1993, pp. 2–3). Europe and European law, are not well defined. As we have already seen, human rights are ill-defined, 'subsidiarity' is famously ambiguous, so is 'citizenship' and 'democracy'. The very status of European law in domestic UK law is ill-defined. Similar examples abound at the micro-level. Thus as we saw in chapters 6 and 7, there is no certain definition even of 'worker', 'spouse' or 'family'. Sophie

Boyron has recently suggested that a similar problem afflicts the concept of 'proportionality', which is not only unfamiliar in the UK, but untranslatable (Boyron, 1992). Francis Snyder concludes that the contradictions in European agricultural law resulted from a particular failure, on the part of both lawyers and politicians, to identify what 'agriculture' was supposed to mean in its European context. He makes a similar observation with regard to the term 'distortion of competition', the indeterminacy of which, he suggests, served to prevent the development of a rational and consistent competition jurisprudence (Snyder, 1990). This particular failing was emphasised in chapter 3.

As we saw in the chapters in Part II of this book, the biggest failures of identity in the European Union are undoubtedly constitutional. There has always been a certain ambivalence, if not anxiety, about self-determination and self-identification of the new European 'Union'. Yet it seems to be a strangely offhand anxiety. For decades there was a European 'Community'. There still is. But now, as well, there is a European 'Union'. But this, of course, is merely a substitute term, one that nobody actually wanted. The 'Union' is an unwanted child, and unloved. The text that everybody wanted at Maastricht, apart from the UK, Portugal and perhaps Denmark, was a European 'Federation', or perhaps 'Confederation'. But what does the 'Union' actually connote, as opposed to a mere 'Community'? Clearly, it seeks to describe something that is more than a common market. But equally clearly, it is not the political union that the currently dominant 'idea' of Europe has sought to realise. Robert Ladrech suggests that the phrase 'an ever closer Union', which finally replaced the presence of federalism in the original Dutch draft of the Maastricht Treaty, symbolised the conscious lack of identity in the European constitutional order. There is, he suggests, a total lack of identity. There is also, he implies, a 'silence', both constitutionally and jurisprudentially. Europe is characterised by a chronic 'underdevelopment of a political discourse'. As I suggested in chapter 2, this underdevelopment is all the more acute in the UK, amongst both the intellectual and lawyer elite, but also amongst the popular interest. The two silences, Ladrech stresses, are not coincidental. Rather, they are both the result of, and at the same time themselves contribute to, not only a lack of identity, but also a lack of interest. Lack of familiarity breeds both distrust and disinterest (Ladrech, 1993, pp. 57–9). As Anthony Smith has recently questioned:

> It is one thing for elites in Brussels, Strasbourg and some European capitals to identify with and work for a united Europe, quite another to attribute such sentiments and beliefs to the great mass of the middle and working classes, let alone the surviving peasantries of Southern and Eastern Europe. Whence will they derive a sense of European identity? (Smith, 1992, p. 72)

It is this concern regarding the crushing indifference of so many new Europeans which has led to the renewed debates about citizenship and, more particularly, democracy. As I suggested in chapter 5, the concentration of the debate on citizenship and democracy actually serves to evade many of the broader questions which the crisis of modernism asks. However, the urgency of the problem, of the failure of identity, which underpins the debate cannot be denied. Weiler suggests that it will not be possible to effect a European Community/Union identity and then a greater interest and trust amongst the peoples of Europe, unless there is a 'transformation' in its democratic appearance (Weiler, 1991, p. 1403). Philip Raworth has perceptively allied the problems of identity and democracy that remain in the post-Maastricht Europe:

> The persistence of national particularism reflects a Community consciousness that is lacking or at least in its infancy. Thus, Parliament is as yet an idiosyncratic body incorporating a European identity that is still artificial. This artificiality is well illustrated by the discrepancy between Parliament's enthusiasm for a federal European state, and the more reserved attitude of the national electorates that became apparent during the ratification of the Maastricht Treaty. (Raworth, 1994, pp. 22–3)

Democracy is still silent in the post-Maastricht Europe, and the failure of identity is the inevitable result of this silence.

The problem of identity is, thus, a constitutional and

jurisprudential failure. As Helen Wallace has emphasised, without some form of constitutional settlement there cannot be the necessary 'collective identity' to which people can be expected to 'express commitment'. The Maastricht Treaty has done nothing to clarify the constitutional position (Wallace, 1993, pp. 100–4). The lack of a legal personality, or constitutional identity, remains, as Ulrich Everling has emphasised, the overriding weakness of the Union structure (Everling, 1992). The weight of legal concern, as we have already seen, is considerable. Most vociferously, Deirdre Curtin has observed that the new 'Union' only serves to retard the identification of a European constitution. In her damning critique of Maastricht, she berates the failure to address the problem of constitutional identity. The Union, she suggests, is 'a loose tarpaulin-like structure . . . suspended artificially and tenuously above' the Community, betraying 'more of a bricoleur's amateurism than a master-bricklayer's strive for perfection and attention to detail'. The Community, she continues, is being 'destroyed', and the 'whole future and credibility of the Communities as a cohesive legal unit which confers rights on individuals and which enters into their national legal systems as an integral part of those systems, is at stake' (Curtin, 1993, pp. 23–4, 67).

Joseph Weiler has suggested two alternative visions which could be adopted in order to effect a constitutional identity in Europe. The first is a federal identity, which he terms 'Europe as Unity', and the second is an intergovernmental identity, which he terms 'Europe as Community'. At present, the Maastricht 'Union' cannot be properly identified with either option. In order for a choice to be made, or indeed, for any constitutional order to be identified in the future, there is, he emphasises, an urgent need to create a European 'discourse' (Weiler, 1991b, pp. 431–7). The viability of certain federal models was discussed in chapter 1. None of them really works, and as Ladrech suggests, few now really advocate a federal model as a perfect 'fit' for Europe (Ladrech, 1993, pp. 61–4). As Theo Koopmans has emphasised, the crucial failing with any mooted federal model is that which pervades contemporary debate surrounding the constitutional jurisprudence of the new Europe as a whole, the question of sovereignty (Koopmans, 1992).

In the UK, as we saw in chapter 4, this concern is little short of a political obsession. Clearly the European Union to some degree requires a transference of constitutional sovereignty. Lord Denning's so-called 'dexterous revolution' no longer deceives. The critical question now is what shape a constitutional jurisprudence not founded on sovereignty can take. The need to look outside existing theories of sovereignty has been suggested by an increasingly large number of commentators. Bruno de Witte has suggested that the 'challenge ahead is to make out of the national constitutions building blocks of European unity rather than bulwarks of sovereignty' (de Witte, 1991, p. 22). The most pressing statement is perhaps that of Neil MacCormick, who has urged us to move 'beyond' sovereignty and suggested that to 'escape from the idea that all law must originate in a single power source, like a sovereign, is thus to discover the possibility of taking a broader, more diffuse, view of the law'. Law 'beyond' sovereignty and 'beyond' modernism can liberate jurisprudence and the law of European integration. This is not to suggest revolution. It is merely to acknowledge the reality of today's Europe:

> Taking the view of the sovereign state which I have suggested, or any reasonable variant of its terms, it seems obvious that no state in Western Europe any longer is a sovereign state. None is in a position such that all the power exercised internally in it, whether politically or legally, derives from purely internal sources. (MacCormick, 1993, pp. 8, 16)

I would suggest that the acknowledgement that we must now attempt to look 'beyond' sovereignty requires us to look beyond the kinds of alternatives presented by Weiler, and towards a third 'vision'. Hannah Arendt, in an earlier appeal for a post-war polity 'beyond sovereignty', suggested that such a movement would identify itself as being post-modern (Arendt, 1972). This third 'vision' is, thus, a distinctively post-modern vision, a vision beyond modernism, and it is this vision which I want to present in the second part of this final chapter.

2 REWRITING POST-MODERN POLITICAL IDENTITIES

What we have not done so far is 'identify' post-modernism. Such an attempt is, of course, the ultimately 'absurd' act (cf. Camus, 1975). Post-modernism identifies identification as critical, and denies its possibility. All that we can do is identify certain post-modern texts and thereby certain characteristics which we may, then, if we wish, term post-modern. Contemporary exponents of post-modernism are legion. I would, however, suggest that there are three which stand out and which are of particular interest in our present engagement with the new Europe, and the possibility of a new European polity. The three names are those of Jean-François Lyotard, Jacques Derrida and Richard Rorty. We have already referred to each of them in previous chapters. Of the three, the name perhaps most readily associated with post-modernism in the wider intellectual world is that of Lyotard. In his *The Postmodern Condition,* Lyotard openly advocated the virtues of post-modernist aesthetics over modernist technology. The former, he suggested, 'reflects' upon, and 'respects', the particular, whilst the latter is engaged in a dehumanising 'totalising' of the human condition. Textually, this totalisation is revealed in the championing of 'metanarratives' (Lyotard, 1984b). The critique of 'metanarratives', and their denial of difference and of the particular, was further developed in *The Differend.* A 'differend' is determined as an incommensurable difference (Lyotard, 1988). The crucial characteristic of post-modernism is that, in contrast with modernism, it is content with difference. There is no anxiety to find basic truths which can serve to determine identity. Post-modernism champions difference.

In *The Differend,* Lyotard determines post-modernism as an innately jurisprudential ambition. The reality of the 'differend' demands a plurality or 'multiplicity of justices' (cf. Lyotard, 1984a, p. 5). As one commentator, David Carroll, has observed, what this 'implies' is 'that judgments must continually be made and remade and that neutrality is impossible' (Carroll, 1984, p. 76). Lyotard's concentration on the idea of 'judgment' as the foundation of justice, as opposed to 'reason' alone, is, of course, a very conscious echo of Immanuel Kant's later writings. In his third *Critique, of*

Judgement, Kant introduced judgement as a complement to pure practical reason and as an idea upon which could be founded the '*sensus communis*' (Lyotard, 1992, pp. 1–25). In section 40 of the *Critique*, Kant defined the *sensus communis* under which

> is to be understood the idea of a public sense, i.e. a critical faculty which in its reflective act takes account (*a priori*) of the mode of representation of everyone else, in order, as it were, to weigh its judgement with the collective reason of mankind .... This is accomplished by weighing the judgement, not so much with the actual, as with the merely possible, judgements of others, and by putting ourselves in the position of everyone else, as the result of a mere abstraction from the limitations which contingently affect our own estimate .... Now it may seem that this operation of reflection is too artificial to be attributed to the faculty which we call common sense. But this is an appearance due only to its expression in abstract formulae. In itself nothing is more natural than to abstract from charm and emotion where one is looking for judgement intended to serve as a universal rule. (Kant, 1991, pp. 151–2)

A number of commentators have recently joined Lyotard in suggesting that a whole new and distinctively post-modern jurisprudence might be developed from Kant's third *Critique* and its concentration on the judgement of the particular. Thus Paul Crowther suggests that a post-modern politics can emerge founded upon an aesthetics of (subjective) judgement, as opposed to a pure ethics of (objective) morality (Crowther, 1993). Similarly Paul Guyer has emphasised Kant's recourse to aesthetics as being an intensely political, and indeed ethical, activity, precisely because it places the cognitive individual at the heart of the activity of judgement (Guyer, 1993). Post-modernism is about retrieving the idea of judgement, and, with it, reinvesting our entire understanding of justice.

Auschwitz represents a particular symbol for Lyotard, as it does in so much post-modern thinking. It, he suggests, represented the ultimate totalising ambition, and thus, the final negation of the modern humanist ethic. Such totalisation, he affirms, sought to 'silence' the excluded. After Auschwitz, according to Lyotard, there can only be 'sentences'. Universalist idealism is dead. In a lecture given at Vienna on the subject of Auschwitz and Heidegger, Lyotard made one of his rare forays into political discourse and suggested that the attempt to 'totalise' a political Europe shared the same ambition as Hitler's, to expunge difference and to 'silence'. Europe was becoming a 'metanarrative', which, as he noted, was a supreme irony, precisely because the original impulse behind the present European 'idea' was to rebuild a Europe in which difference would not only be acknowledged, but would be respected, and in which there could never be another Auschwitz (Lyotard, 1993a). It is these views which we can hear echoed in Lyotard's human rights lecture, 'The Other's Rights', which was introduced in the previous chapter. It was in this lecture that Lyotard once again emphasised the centrality of justice and, most particularly, justice as respect for the 'other'. The key to effecting this 'respect' lay in preserving the participatory potential of dialogue. To have voice is to be empowered; to be 'silenced' is to be marginalised and excluded (Lyotard, 1993b). The new Europe must be written in such a way that it ensures the active dialogic participation of each and every individual who resides within its boundaries.

We have also encountered Jacques Derrida. As we saw in chapter 1, it was Derrida who, in his essay 'The Other Heading', sought to deconstruct the idea of Europe. It was the ahistoricality of this idea which Derrida challenged. What it revealed, he suggested, above all, was a failure of identity and denial of difference. Like Lyotard, he suggested that Europe was trying to present itself as some sort of metanarrative, founded upon a dominion of cultural and economic homogeneity (Derrida, 1992). This is a textual play. Like Lyotard, Derrida is most renowned for his championing of the text, because he too suggests that, in the post-modern world, following the death of humanist ethics, there can be only textual ethics. A post-modern ethics, he suggested, perhaps most powerfully in *Of Spirit: Heidegger and the Question*, will be one which respects the textuality of difference. It is one which empowers the voice of the 'silenced' against the totalising ambitions of modernism. Again, as with

Lyotard, for Derrida the epitome of modern humanism was Hitler's Germany. The epitomic text was the 1933 Freiburg '*Rektorat*', Heidegger's tortuous attempt to champion a universalising *Geist* as a philosophical apologia for Nazism (Derrida, 1989). Deconstruction of a text, Derrida stresses, is merely the prelude to a textual-ethical reconstruction. Concentration on difference and on the particular is not thus nihilistic, as so often is alleged. Indeed, it is the totalising impulse of modernism which is nihilistic. Auschwitz was the epitome of modernity and of nihilism. Deconstruction of any text, according to Derrida, will reveal its implicit codes. It will recognise what is identified in the text and what is silenced and left 'outside' the text. The ambition of the post-modern ethic is to reintroduce the excluded and to empower the particular.

Again like Lyotard, Derrida sees post-modernism and deconstruction as particularly jurisprudential exercises. The ambition of both, in a sense the only ambition, is to describe justice. In his essay 'The Force of Law', Derrida emphasised that the 'force' of law is the product of the necessary 'difference' between the 'we' and the 'other', those with voice (and text) and those silenced and powerless. Law is thus a 'differential force'. In aligning textual deconstruction with political power 'differentials', Derrida is explicitly approving the textual turn in Critical Legal Studies. His concentration on the 'deconstructibility' of justice, as opposed to the undeconstructibility of law, serves to emphasise still further its ethical component. Law has nothing to do with justice, which is itself an 'obligation' owed to the 'other'. A post-modern jurisprudence, he affirms, is a jurisprudence which forever deconstructs the pretended universalism of any philosophy of law and any constitutional order. A properly critical jurisprudence is the championing of the particular, and a complementary openness to that which lies 'beyond' and which has yet to be realised (Derrida, 1990).

A substantive post-modern jurisprudence has yet to establish itself. Post-modernism, it is often suggested, can be better described as 'approaching' or 'confronting' law (Hunt, 1990). Whilst the most recent 'approaches' have tended to concentrate primarily on textualism and psychoanalysis, the political import of post-modernism is familiar. The critique of universalism and technology, the pluralism, the advocacy of alternative forms of participatory democracy, the concern for difference, for the excluded and silenced, the politics implicit and explicit in the writings of such as Lyotard and Derrida are, of course, ideas and concepts familiar to the legal audience in the writings of the Critical Legal Studies movement. They are also the ideas and concepts which lie at the heart of many of the chapters in this book. A more overtly political post-modern 'approach' cannot be distinguished in its origins from CLS, and if a genetic association is suggested, it is that post-modern jurisprudence seeks to go 'beyond' CLS (Douzinas et al., 1994; Goodrich, 1992).

Arguably, the most concerted and substantive attempt to date to present a post-modern political jurisprudence, is Drucilla Cornell's. It was Cornell's application of post-modernism to feminist legal studies which, I suggested in chapter 7, could provide a theoretical foundation for a post-modern European sex equality law. Cornell has developed her post-modern jurisprudence almost exclusively from Derrida. Her primary determination is to stress the ethical reconstructive potential of deconstructionism. What she terms the 'philosophy of the limit' is a philosophy which identifies boundaries and moves 'beyond' them so as to acknowledge the discourse of those initially excluded by the 'limits' of modernism; 'those' includes women. What she ultimately advocates is 'dialogism', from which can be developed a post-modern 'ethic of citizenship'. It is an expression of pluralism and of participatory democracy complemented by a conception of identity which is reflectively determinable and fluid and which, rather than threatening difference, actually nourishes it. A post-modern polity is one which is founded upon difference and upon 'transformative' discursive participation (Cornell, 1992).

Another who has attempted to define the boundaries of a post-modern polity, and to give the post-modernism a more solid political edge, is Richard Rorty. It is this more overtly political commentary which has made Rorty such an inspiration for North American CLS writers. The later Rorty has increasingly abandoned the hermeneutic conversationalism which so attracted him in his *Philosophy and the Mirror of Nature*, in favour of the more deconstructive ironic conversationalism of such as Derrida (Rorty, 1980; 1989, pp. 122–37). His self-appointed task is to translate these ironic textual-ethical insights into the political arena. The ambition is to accommodate all the dualities which pervade contemporary political philosophy; freedom and truth, private and public, irony and solidarity. This accommodation will realise a liberal utopia which will be narrative rather than theoretical, and created and self-asserted rather than discovered. Such a utopia will articulate a philosophy of what Rorty terms 'post-modern bourgeois liberalism'. The twin pillars of this post-modern bourgeois liberalism are the reality of political contingency and conversational solidarity. Like Cornell, Rorty suggests that a post-modern liberal polity will be conversationally constructed, and will, then, reflect the ethics of a constructively rational community. Such a community, he suggests, always 'respects' difference. It is, indeed, defined by difference. Such a community will also encapsulate a radical decentralisation of power, together with the constructive conversational participation of everyone. It will, he urges, 'revitalise' democracy. As we saw in the previous chapter, such a revitalisation can equally be applied to our understanding of human rights. Political freedom in the contingent community is the freedom to converse and to persuade, and thus to construct. It is also the freedom to be listened to. The essentially 'human' right is the right to this idea of freedom (Rorty, 1989, chs. 1–3). Accordingly, Rorty suggests:

> A liberal society is one whose ideal can be fulfilled by persuasion rather than force, by reform rather than revolution, by the free and open encounters of present linguistic and other practices with suggestions for new practices. But this is to say that an ideal liberal society is one which has no purpose except freedom, no goal except a willingness to see how such encounters go and to abide by the outcome. It has no purpose except to make life easier for poets and revolutionaries while seeing to it that they make life harder for others only by words, and not deeds. It is a society whose hero is the strong poet and the revolutionary because it recognizes that it is what it is, has the morality it has, speaks the language it does,

> not because it approximates the will of God or the nature of man but because certain poets and revolutionaries of the past spoke as they did. To see one's language, one's conscience, one's morality, and one's highest hopes as contingent products, as liberalizations of what once were accidentally produced metaphors, is to adopt a self-identity which suits one for citizenship in such an ideally liberal state. (ibid., pp. 60–1)

Aside from merely presenting his own vision of a textual post-modern liberalism, Rorty seeks to expropriate others. The heroes of the liberal polity are the 'strong poets'. Such a poet is one who merely describes and redescribes, critically aware that any truth is their truth, and merely a textual truth. John Rawls, he suggests, is precisely such a poet. According to Rorty, the later Rawls, specifically the Rawls of the 'Overlapping Consensus', is a different, more critical and more enlightened Rawls. His is an ironic politics, which recognises that moral principles are only of value in relation to specific institutional and practical solutions, and can only be determined as a communicative morality. The abandonment of 'comprehensive' theory has indeed characterised the later Rawls. As he claims in his recent *Political Liberalism*:

> [Political liberalism] leads to the idea of a political conception of justice as a free standing view starting from the fundamental ideas of democratic society and presupposing no particular wider doctrine. We put no doctrinal obstacles to its winning allegiance to itself, so that it can be supported by a reasonable and enduring overlapping consensus. (Rawls, 1993a, p. 40)

The 'political liberalism' which Rawls now espouses is, as we saw in the previous chapter, constructed around three 'fundamental concepts'. The first is pluralism. The second is reasonableness as a substantively intersubjective concept. Democratic society, Rawls tells us, is determined by the demands of a 'reasonable pluralism'. What is particularly important here is Rawls concentration on rewriting, as an echo of Lyotard and Derrida, a determination of judgement. The 'sources' of judgement, he suggests, are experimental, social, political and historical. Judgement is always contingent, and is the concept to be used in the contingencies of the political situation (ibid., pp. 56–7). The third fundamental is constructivism. We construct our society and our morality. The purpose of the much vaunted overlapping consensus is not only to accommodate pluralism and to stabilise it, but also to construct 'moral' consensus. The nature of Rawls' new liberalism, and the extent to which it enjoys a closer alignment to that of such as Rorty, as opposed to his own earlier writings, is seen in his concluding observations in *Political Liberalism*:

> The conception of justice to which these principles belong is not to be regarded as a method of answering the jurists' questions, but as a guiding framework which, if jurists find it convincing, may orient their reflections, complement their knowledge, and assist their judgment. We must not ask too much of a philosophical view. A conception of justice fulfils its social role provided that persons equally conscientious and sharing roughly the same beliefs find that, by affirming the framework of deliberation set up by it, they are normally led to a sufficient convergence of judgment necessary to achieve effective and fair social cooperation. (ibid., p. 368)

This is a jurisprudence of the particular, a jurisprudence of difference and respect, and of pluralism and participation. Might this not be a jurisprudence appropriate for the new Europe? I would suggest that it is.

3 THE NEW EUROPE AS A POST-MODERN POLITY

I would further suggest that the writings of such as Lyotard, Derrida, Cornell, Rorty and Rawls represent a kind of consensus for the need to rewrite political and legal thought in line with the demands of the new post-modern era. There is a consensus that we must attain an understanding which is 'beyond' universalism, and which respects the particular, which aims to realise the cherished ideals of genuine participatory democracy, which seeks to reclaim power from ruling and intellectual elites, whose inadequacies are becoming all too obvious and which is directed to framing a new identity founded on social solidarity. A post-modern polity is one in which everyone is not only belonging, but is felt to belong. At present, we no longer enjoy such identities. Echoing the comments of Jacques Derrida, Anthony Smith has suggested that the attempt to erase cultural heterogeneity in the new Europe, merely creates an identity vacuum. There is no alternative cultural homogeneity. There is no such thing as a 'European', at least not in a cultural sense (Smith, 1992). There is a crisis of belonging, not just in a European sense, but equally in a domestic sense. People trust Westminster or Paris or Bonn little more than they trust Brussels or Strasbourg. There is a very real 'crisis of governance' in the new Europe, and it is particularly acute in the new Union (Lodge, 1993, p. 383). Joseph Weiler refers to a 'legitimacy crisis' which is particularly apparent in the new Europe. It is a Europe in which people do not see themselves as 'belonging' (Weiler, 1991b, pp. 416–19). Soledad Garcia has emphasised the extent to which the problem of legitimacy is at once a problem of identity and belonging, and in words which strongly resonate with the kind of post-modern liberalism espoused by Rorty, stresses, 'Europe will exist as an unquestionable political community only when European identity permeates people's lives and daily existence. This will require a truly European civil society' (Garcia, 1993, p. 15).

More optimistically, Attracta Ingram has intimated that the new Europe represents precisely such an opportunity for the exercise of a post-modern polity. Echoing the post-modernism of Rorty and Rawls, she suggests that the key lies in realising a European Union 'founded on liberal justice', which takes us 'beyond' the liberalism of the nation-state. A post-modern liberalism must radically decentralise power from the nation-state and relocate it at its most basic societal level. A European identity can only be effected if national identity is erased. There must be, she concludes, a 'self-defining European us' (Ingram, 1993). We must define the new Europe, so that, as Paul Howe has suggested, it reflects the multiplicity of identities which characterise the post-modern world. It should no longer be 'an' identity determined by intellectual and political elites, for intellectual and political elites. Modern liberalism, he further suggests, is defined by its appreciation of multiple identities and the complementary need for the dispersion and decentralisation of power (Howe, 1995). The reduction of the nation-state, as the previous chapters have repeatedly suggested, is vital if a new Europe is to be realised.

This does not necessarily mean the annihilation of the nation-state. Indeed, it is hard to imagine a Europe not determined by nation-states, and, as we saw in chapter 3, the idea that the nation-states might somehow dissolve in the face of the idea of an integrated Europe remains little more than a mythology. European integration remains strictly bounded by the limits of nation-state power (cf. Horsman & Marshall, 1995, p. 264). Anthony Smith has advocated a distinctly post-national and post-modern model for a new Europe, which shares many of the theoretical assumptions of such as Rorty, Rawls, Ingram and Howe. He suggests a 'voluntaristic and pluralistic conception' of the nation-state, which we can regard as 'a rational association of common laws and culture within a defined territory'. Such a definition complements what he terms a Europe of 'multiple identities', in which each individual identifies not just with Europe and with a nation-state, but also with a multiplicity of other geographical, social, economic, religious, cultural and historical identities. Every identity, he affirms, including a national identity, is in fact made up of constituent identities. A European identity will be no exception. Borrowing from Wittgenstein, he refers to a 'family of cultures', which can enjoy a Rawlsian 'overlapping' political culture, which can cut across any pretended boundaries or margins. Such an identity, he concludes, 'will be both distinctive and inclusive, differentiating yet assimilative' (Smith, 1992, pp. 56–60, 70–1, 76).

Horsman and Marshall describe a similar Europe, which they term 'high modern'. In using this particular terminology they wish to emphasise the paradox of a situation in which the post-modern at once represents an intensification of the modern, and a denial of it: the classical deconstructionist feint (Horsman & Marshall, 1995, pp. 267–8). Such a Europe, they suggest, will be part of a new world order geared to the better 'management of capital' in the cause of protecting the margins of society. Such a post-modern/high modern Europe would, of course, be one characterised by a fragmentation of identity, and thus one in which there was a corresponding proliferation of margins. In an eloquent passage, they suggest that:

> The trick will be to make democracy work, and to place the citizen at the centre of politics. The citizen may find that local government is the most appealing of his options, but he will have to be encouraged to pay allegiance to other policy-making levels too: regional and international. In all these spheres, one of the central problems will be deciding how authority can be located . . . It is a question of deciding how powerful supranational organizations should be, how their work will be made accountable to the citizen, how much power must be sensibly devolved to a level closer to the individual. The difficulty arises because the edges of societies and markets are eroding and are less easy to draw on a map. New boundaries are needed; new ways of dividing the tasks of government; new ways of relating the diverse interests and concerns of citizens. . . . These boundaries are not just a question of an organizing principle but a principle of legitimacy. The weakening of nation-states makes finding a single national purpose, a national interest, more difficult. Multiple loyalties, and the right system to arbitrate among them, must be addressed. (ibid., pp. 266–7)

I have also suggested repeatedly that the potential key for unlocking such a realisation might be the much maligned and much misunderstood idea of subsidiarity. The determination to evade a definition of subsidiarity, both at Maastricht and afterwards, makes the idea a peculiarly post-modern one. For some, as we have seen, subsidiarity is supposed to enhance the position of the nation-state, whilst for others, it is seen to be a mechanism for the liberation of the individual and the complemetary radical dispersion of power, politically, socially and economically, as well as geographically (Picht, 1993, pp. 92–3). It may thus emerge into the light as a genuinely post-modern incarnation of difference as justice, or, alternatively, it may turn out to be technology which will enforce the further marginalisation of the particular. Of course, it may never emerge into the light at all (Garcia & Wallace, 1993, p. 174).

The resolution of subsidiarity may thus be uncertain, but its potential should not be denied. I have already suggested how it may represent a means of thinking constitutionally without necessarily founding our thoughts on the sanctity of sovereignty. I have also suggested how such a determination chimes with the ideas of participatory democracy, how it may be seen as an instrument for the empowerment of women, and, indeed, all those effectively marginalised in the new Europe. I have also already discussed the idea that subsidiarity may be a mechanism for realising greater industrial democracy, as suggested by such as the Workers' Council directives. A further, and very obvious, way in which subsidiarity may be able to effect a greater dispersal of power in a multilayered Europe is with its employment in regional democracy. Subsidiarity, it has been suggested, might finally realise the very post-modern idea of a 'Europe of the regions' (Peterson, 1994, pp. 118–19, 123–9). Certainly the philosophy of regionalism is both liberal and post-modern in the sense we have just defined in the previous section. Joseph Weiler has talked of a regional policy enhancing 'democracy in the sense of giving people more direct control of areas of public policy which affect their life' (Weiler, 1991b, p. 185) Christopher Harvie has recently echoed Denis de Rougemont's definition of regionalism in the new European context, as being 'the space for civic participation in which man comes alive to the world and to himself at the same time' (Harvie, 1994, pp. 6–10). The idea of 'civic' participation has obviously liberal connotations, and there is a danger, as Harvie observes, that regionalism can remain squarely in the thrall of the nation-states and thus the middle-class, pseudo-nationalist elites who enjoy dominion in these states (ibid., pp. 54–9, 66–8). However, the idea of civil participation can also be interpreted as defining the essence of the Rortian utopia. Harvie further suggests that the foundations of liberal regionalist philosophy can be found in the writings of those early twentieth-century English pluralists whom we considered in chapter 5 as the possible intellectual progenitors of a participatory European democracy (ibid., p. 14).

Although there is, then, an intellectual determination of regionalism – indeed, there are diametrically opposite determinations – regionalism has always been redefined in Community politics, as regional development. This development definition, in turn, has always tended to be relegated behind wider economic ambitions. Regionalism has not necessarily been seen first as a mechanism for realising more effective democracy, and regional democracy has been enhanced only to the extent that it might assist the Community in creating economic wealth. As Joanne Scott has recently re-emphasised, regionalism has only recently returned to the centre-stage of European politics because the Cecchini Report suggested that the absence of some regional dispersion of economic power was costing everybody, the nation-states included, money. There has, she suggests, been a wilful 'indifference' on the part of the Community to the social and cultural contexts of regionalism. The Commission thus waxes lyrically about the possible benefits of enhanced local participation in Community government, but as yet has effected little. Subsidiarity offers the possibility of an effective dispersion of political, social and economic power on a regional basis. Although at the same time, as Scott acknowledges, it might just as easily be interpreted, in its present guise, as threatening the re-entrenchment of the nation-state against the regions. As ever, everything will depend on how subsidiarity is perceived in action (Scott, 1995, pp. 10–11, 21, 30–3, 56–60).

According to Laurent Fabius, former President of the French National Assembly, the ambition of the new Europe must be

> to move beyond the traditional forms of Community. In this respect the European Community would appear to foreshadow a more general movement. Where our nations are concerned, states are increasingly integrated into wider structures, while nation states at the same time show a growing trend toward devolution. (Ladrech, 1993, pp. 66–7)

For Fabius, it seems, the process of dismantling modern Europe has already begun, and the complementary process of creating a post-modern Europe is upon us. Geoffrey Howe has made a similar observation, suggesting that the new Europe reveals the truth that the modern nation-state is no longer 'absolute', and that there is a pressing need for a politics which can accommodate the disintegration of homogeneity and counter the reactionary threat of nationalism (G. Howe, 1995). The similarity between these statements, from two respected conservative politicians, and those of such as MacCormick, and the post-modern political utopias of such as Rorty and Cornell, is striking. If they are right, then the 'totalising' ambitions of the European 'idea' are also destined to fall, and so is its jurisprudence. Horsman and Marshall describe a 'bonfire of the certainties' (Horsman & Marshall, 1995, p. 267). In the place of modernist certainties there can be a Europe which cherishes an identity of difference, a Europe which triumphs the particular and the individual, a Europe in which the margins of power and wealth are erased, and in which no one is excluded or silenced. It will be a Europe which acknowledges its history. It will most importantly be a Europe 'beyond' the nation-state, and in which power is radically dispersed, regionally, socially, economically. It will, in turn, be a Europe in which the law is integrated in the cause of justice and which appreciates the virtue of a constitution beyond sovereignty. It will be a Europe which accommodates alternative forms of political discourse, in which democracy can be redefined as participatory and citizenship as social. It will be a Europe in which there is no marginalised underclass and in which sex equality can become a socially structural reality, not a mere rhetorical feint. Finally, it will become a Europe in which human rights can be realised as the construction of all its inhabitants. Such a Europe will enjoy a distinctive identity. It will itself be different, and it will be defined by difference. This is a post-modern vision of Europe.

Case List

Belgium 32/87 [1989] ECR 997
Bettray 344/87 [1989] ECR 1621
Bilka-Kaufhaus 170/84 [1986] ECR 1607
Bostock 2/92 judgment 24 March 1994
Brind [1991] 1 All ER 720
Bulmer [1974] 2 All ER 1226
Cinéthèque 60–1/84 [1985] ECR 2605
Costa 6/64 [1964] ECR 585
Cunningham [1991] 4 All ER 310
Defrenne 43/75 [1976] ECR 455 & 149/77 [1978] ECR 1365
Demirel 112/86 [1987] ECR 3719
Diatta 267/83 [1985] ECR 567
Doody [1993] 3 WLR 154
Factortame 213/89 [1990] ECR I–2433 & [1991] 1 All ER 70
Francovich 6 & 9/90 [1991] ECR I–5357
Gebroeders Beentjes 31/87 [1988] ECR 4635
Grogan 159/90 [1991] ECR I–4685
Hauer 44/79 [1979] ECR 3727
Heylens 222/86 [1987] ECR 4097
In re M [1993] 3 WLR 433
Internationale Handelsgesellschaft 11/70 [1970] ECR 1125
Klensch 201–2/85 [1986] ECR 1339
M v Home Office [1992] 4 All ER 97
Macarthy's 129/79 [1979] ECR 1275 & [1981] QB 180
Nold no. 2 4/73 [1974] ECR 491
Peterborough [1991] 4 All ER 192
Reed 59/85 [1986] ECR 1629
Rutili 36/75 [1975] ECR 1219
Sandhu [1982] 2 CMLR 553
Simmenthal 106/77 [1978] ECR 629
Stauder 29/69 [1969] ECR 419
Torfaen 145/88 [1989] ECR 3851
Van Duyn 41/74 [1974] ECR 1337
Wachauf 5/88 [1989] ECR 2609
Walters [1993] 26 HLR 170
Woodpulp 89, 104, 114, 116–17 & 125–9/85 [1985] ECR 5193

References

Ackers, L. (1994) 'Women, Citizenship and European Community Law: The Gender Implications of the Free Movement of Persons', *Journal of Social Welfare and Family Law,* 391–406.

Alderman, R. & Carter, N. (1991) 'A Very Tory Coup: The Ousting of Mrs. Thatcher', *Parliamentary Affairs,* 44, 1128–33.

Allan, T. (1983) 'Parliamentary Sovereignty: Lord Denning's Dexterous Revolution', *Oxford Journal of Legal Studies,* 3, 22–33.

Allan, T. (1992) *Law, Liberty and Justice: The Legal Foundations of the British Constitution* (Oxford: Clarendon Press).

Allott, P. (1991) 'The European Community is Not the True European Community', *Yale Law Journal* 100, 2485–500.

Anav, G. (1989) 'Parliamentary Sovereignty: An Anachronism?', *Columbia Journal of Transnational Law,* 27, 631–56.

Anderson, M. den Boer, M. & Millar, G. (1994) 'European Citizenship and Cooperation in Justice and Home Affairs', in A. Duff, J. Pinder & R. Pryce (eds.), *Maastricht and Beyond: Building the European Union* (London: Routledge).

Arendt, H. (1951a) *Antisemitism* (New York: Harcourt Brace Jovanovich).

Arendt, H. (1951b) *Imperialism* (New York: Harcourt Brace Jovanovich).

Arendt, H. (1951c) *Totalitarianism* (New York: Harcourt Brace Jovanovich).

Arendt, H. (1963) *Eichmann in Jerusalem: A Report on the Banality of Evil* (Harmondsworth: Penguin).

Arendt, H. (1972) *Crises of the Republic* (New York: Harcourt Brace Jovanovich).

Arendt, H. (1982) *Lectures on Kant's Political Philosophy* (Chicago: Chicago University Press).

Armstrong, H., Taylor, J. & Williams, R. (1994) 'Regional Policy', in M. Artis & N. Lee (eds.), *The Economics of the European Union* (Oxford: Oxford University Press).

Artis, M. (1992) 'The Maastricht Road to Monetary Union', *Journal of Common Market Studies,* 30, 299–309.

Baldwin-Edwards, M. (1991) 'Immigration after 1992', *Policy and Politics,* 19, 199–211.

Balkin, J. (1987) 'Deconstructive Practice and Legal Theory', *Yale Law Journal,* 96, 743–86.

Bauboeck, R. (1991) 'Migration and Citizenship', *New Community,* 18, 27–48.

Bengoetxea, J. (1993) *The Legal Reasoning of the European Court of Justice* (Oxford: Clarendon Press).

Bermann, G. (1984) 'The Single European Act: A New Constitution for the Community', *Columbia Journal of Transnational Law,* 27, 529–87.

Bibas, S. (1992) 'The European Court of Justice and the US Supreme Court: Parallels in Fundamental Rights Jurisprudence', *Hastings International and Comparative Law Review,* 15, 253–95.

Bieber, R., Pantalis, J. & Schoo, J. (1986) 'Implications of the Single Act for the European Parliament', *Common Market Law Review*, 23, 767–92.

Bingham, T. (1993) 'The European Convention on Human Rights: Time to Incorporate', *Law Quarterly Review*, 109, 390–400.

Boyle, J. (1985) 'The Politics of Reason: Critical Legal Theory and Local Social Thought', *University of Pennsylvania Law Review*, 133, 685–780.

Boyron, S. (1992) 'Proportionality in English Administrative Law: A Faulty Translation?', *Oxford Journal of Legal Studies*, 12, 237–64.

Bradley, A. (1994) 'The Sovereignty of Parliament – in Perpetuity?', in J. Jowell & D. Oliver (eds.), *The Changing Constitution* (Oxford: Oxford University Press).

Bulmer, S. (1994) 'History and Institutions of the European Union', in M. Artis & N. Lee (eds.), *The Economics of the European Union* (Oxford: Oxford University Press).

Burgess, G. (1992) *The Politics of the Ancient Constitution* (London: Macmillan).

Campbell, J. Barnes, I. & Pepper, C. (1990) 'Implementing the Internal Market', in C. Crouch & D. Marquand (eds.), *The Politics of 1992: Beyond the Single European Market* (London: Blackwell).

Campbell, N. (1994) 'The Duty to Give Reasons in Administrative Law', *Public Law*, 184–91.

Camus, A. (1975) *The Myth of Sisyphus* (Harmondsworth: Penguin).

Canovan, M. (1992) *Hannah Arendt* (Cambridge: Cambridge University Press).

Cappelletti, M., Seccombe, M. & Weiler, J. (eds.) (1985) *Integration Through Law* (Berlin: de Gruyter).

Cardozo, R. & Corbett, R. (1986) 'The Crocodile Initiative', in J. Lodge, *European Union: The European Community in Search of a Future* (London: St Martin's Press).

Carroll, D. (1984) 'Rephrasing the Political with Kant and Lyotard: From Aesthetic to Political Judgments', *Diacritics*, 14, 74–88.

Carty, A. (1991) 'English Constitutional Law from a Postmodernist Perspective', in P. Fitzpatrick (ed.), *Dangerous Supplements: Resistance and Renewal in Jurisprudence* (London: Pluto Press).

Chalmers, D. (1994) 'Repackaging the Internal Market – The Ramifications of the *Keck* Judgment', *European Law Review*, 19, 385–403.

Churchill, R. & Foster, N. (1987) 'Double Standards in Human Rights? The Treatment of Spanish Fishermen by the European Community', *European Law Review*, 12, 430–43.

Clapham, A. (1990) 'A Human Rights Policy for the European Community', *Yearbook of European Law*, 10, 309–66.

Clarke, P. (1992) 'Margaret Thatcher's Leadership in Historical Perspective', *Parliamentary Affairs*, 45, 1–17.

Closa, C. (1994) 'Citizenship of the European Union and Nationality of Member States', in D. O'Keeffe & P. Twomey (eds.), *Legal Issues of the Maastricht Treaty* (London: Chancery Press).

Closa, C. (1995) 'Citizenship of the Union and Nationality of Member States', *Common Market Law Review*, 32, 487–518.

Close, P. (1995) *Citizenship, Europe and Change* (London: Macmillan).

Cockfield, Lord (1990) 'The Real Significance of 1992', in C. Crouch & D. Marquand (eds.), *The Politics of 1992: Beyond the Single European Market* (London: Blackwell).
Coombes, D. (1994) 'Problems of Governance in the Union', in A. Duff, J. Pinder & R. Pryce (eds.) *Maastricht and Beyond: Building the European Union* (London: Routledge).
Coppel, J. (1993) 'Edinburgh Subsidiarity', *Northern Ireland Legal Quarterly*, 44, 179–87.
Coppel, J. & O'Neill, A. (1992) 'The European Court of Justice: Taking Rights Seriously?' *Legal Studies*, 12, 227–45.
Corbett, R. (1994) 'Representing the People', in A. Duff, J. Pinder & R. Pryce (eds.), *Maastricht and Beyond: Building the European Union* (London: Routledge).
Cornell, D. (1985) 'Toward a Modern/Postmodern Reconstruction of Ethics', *University of Pennsylvania Law Review*, 133, 291–380.
Cornell, D. (1988) 'Institutionalization of Meaning, Recollective Imagination and the Potential for Transformative Legal Interpretation', *University of Pennsylvania Law Review*, 136, 1135–229.
Cornell, D. (1991) *Beyond Accommodation: Ethical Feminism, Deconstruction and the Law* (London: Routledge).
Cornell, D. (1992) *The Philosophy of the Limit* (London: Routledge).
Cornell, D. (1993) *Transformations* (London: Routledge).
Craig, P. (1991) 'Sovereignty of the United Kingdom Parliament after *Factortame*', *Yearbook of European Law*, 11, 221–55.
Craig, P. (1993) '*Francovich*, Remedies and the Scope of Damages Liability', *Law Quarterly Review*, 109, 595–621.
Craig, P. & de Burca, G. (1995) *EC Law: Texts, Cases and Materials* (Oxford: Oxford University Press).
Crowther, P. (1993) *Critical Aesthetics and Postmodernism* (Oxford: Clarendon Press).
Cullen, H. (1994) 'The Subsidiary Woman', *Journal of Social Welfare and Family Law*, 407–21.
Curtin, D. (1993) 'The Constitutional Structure of the Union: A Europe of Bits and Pieces', *Common Market Law Review*, 30, 17–69.
Curtin, D. & Meijers, H. (1995) 'The Principle of Open Government in Schengen and the European Union: Democratic Retrogression?', *Common Market Law Review*, 32, 391–442.
Dallen, R. (1990) 'An Overview of European Community Protection of Human Rights, with Some Special References to the UK', *Common Market Law Review*, 27, 761–90.
Dankert, P. (1982) 'The European Community – Past, Present and Future', *Journal of Common Market Studies*, 21, 3–18.
de Burca, G. (1992) 'Giving Effect to European Community Directives', *Modern Law Review*, 55, 215–40.
de Burca, G. (1993) 'Fundamental Rights and the Reach of EC Law', *Oxford Journal of Legal Studies*, 13, 283–319.
Dehousse, R. (1988) '1992 and Beyond: The Institutional Dimension of the Internal Market Programme', *Legal Issues of European Integration*, 109–36.

Delanty, G. (1995) *Inventing Europe: Idea, Identity, Reality* (London: Macmillan).

Denman, R. (1995) 'Missed Chances: Britain and Europe in the Twentieth Century', *Political Quarterly*, 66, 36–45.

D'Entreves, A. (1987) *Aquinas: Selected Political Writings* (London: Blackwell).

Derrida, J. (1983) 'The Principle of Reason: The University in the Eyes of its Pupils', *Diacritics*, 13, 3–20.

Derrida, J. (1989) *Of Spirit: Heidegger and the Question* (Chicago: Chicago University Press).

Derrida, J. (1990) 'The Force of Law: "The Mystical Foundation of Authority"', *Cardozo Law Review*, 11, 920–1045.

Derrida, J. (1992) *The Other Heading: Reflections on Today's Europe* (Bloomington: Indiana University Press).

de Witte, B. (1991) 'Community Law and National Constitutional Values', *Legal Issues in European Integration*, 1–22.

Docksey, C. (1991) 'The Principle of Equality between Women and Men as a Fundamental Right under Community Law', *Industrial Law Journal*, 20, 258–80.

D'Oliveira, H. (1994) 'Expanding External and Shrinking Internal Borders: Europe's Defence Mechanisms in the Areas of Free Movement, Immigration and Asylum', in D. O'Keeffe & P. Twomey (eds.), *Legal Issues of the Maastricht Treaty* (London: Chancery Press).

Douzinas, C. Goodrich, P. & Hachamovitch, Y. (1994) *Politics, Postmodernity and Critical Legal Studies* (London: Routledge).

Duchenes, F. (1990) 'Less or More than Europe?: European Integration in Retrospect', in C. Crouch & D. Marquand (eds.), *The Politics of 1992: Beyond the Single European Market* (London: Blackwell)

Ehlermann, C. (1990) 'The 1992 Project: Stages, Structures, Results and Prospects', *Michigan Journal of International Law*, 11, 1097–118.

Ehlermann, C. (1992) 'The Contribution of EC Competition Policy to the Single Market', *Common Market Law Review*, 29, 257–82.

Eksteins, M. (1989) *The Rites of Spring* (Toronto: Lester & Orpen Denyss).

Ellis, E. (1991) *European Sex Equality Law* (Oxford: Clarendon Press).

Emiliou, N. (1992) 'Subsidiarity: An Effective Barrier Against "the Enterprises of Ambition"?', *European Law Review*, 17, 383–407.

Emiliou, N. (1994) 'Subsidiarity: Panacea or Fig Leaf?', in D. O'Keeffe & P. Twomey (eds.), *Legal Issues of the Maastricht Treaty* (London: Chancery Press).

Eriksson, L. (1993) 'The Disintegration of the Nation-State', in M. Karlsson (ed.), *Law, Justice and the State* (Berlin: Duncker and Humbolt).

Evans, A. (1991)'Nationality Law and European Integration', *European Law Review*, 16, 190–215.

Everling, U. (1992) 'Reflections on the Structure of the European Union', *Common Market Law Review*, 29, 1053–77.

Fenwick, H. & Hervey, T. (1995) 'Sex Equality in the Single Market: New Directions for the European Court of Justice', *Common Market Law Review*, 32, 443–71.

Fitzpatrick, B. (1992) 'Community Social Law after Maastricht', *Industrial Law Journal*, 21, 199–213.

Foucault, M. (1979) *Discipline and Punish* (Harmondsworth, Penguin).
Frazer, T. (1990) 'Competition Policy after 1992: The Next Step', *Modern Law Review*, 53, 609–23.
Fredman, S. (1992) 'European Community Discrimination Law', *Industrial Law Journal*, 21, 119–34.
Frowein, J. Schulhofer, S. & Shapiro, M. (1986) 'The Protection of Fundamental Human Rights as a Vehicle of Integration', in M. Cappelletti, M. Seccombe & J. Weiler (eds.), *Integration Through Law*, vol. 1 (Berlin: de Gruyter).
Frug, G. (1987) 'Empowering Cities in a Federal System', *Urban Lawyer*, 19, 553–68.
Frug, G. (1990) 'Administrative Democracy', *University of Toronto Law Journal*, 40, 559–86.
Frug, M. (1992) *Postmodern Legal Feminism* (London: Routledge).
Gabel, P. (1980) 'Reification in Legal Reasoning', *Research in Law and Sociology*, 3, 25–51.
Gabel, P. (1984) 'The Phenomenology of Rights-Consciousness and the Pact of the Withdrawn Selves', *Texas Law Review*, 62, 1563–96.
Gabel, P. & Harris, P. (1982) 'Building Power and Breaking Images: Critical Legal Theory and the Practice of Law', *Review of Law and Social Change*, 11, 369–411.
Gabel, P. & Kennedy, D.(1984) 'Roll Over Beethoven', *Stanford Law Review*, 36, 1–55.
Garcia, S. (1993) 'Europe's Fragmented Identities and the Frontiers of Citizenship', in S. Garcia (ed.), *European Identity and the Search for Legitimacy* (London: Pinter).
Garcia, S. & Wallace, H. (1993) 'Conclusion', in S. Garcia (ed.), *European Identity and the Search for Legitimacy* (London: Pinter).
Gasset, O. (1972) *The Revolt of the Masses* (London: Unwin).
Geddes, A. (1995) 'Immigrant and Ethnic Minorities and the EU's "Democratic Deficit"', *Journal of Common Market Studies*, 33, 197–217.
George, S. (1991) *Policy and Politics in the European Community* (Oxford: Oxford University Press).
George, S. (1994) *An Awkward Partner: Britain in the European Community* (Oxford: Oxford University Press).
Gilchrist, J. & Deacon, D. (1990) 'Curbing Subsidies', in P. Montagnon (ed.), *European Competition Policy* (London: PIIA/Pinter).
Goodrich, P. (1992) 'Critical Legal Studies in England: Prospective Histories', *Oxford Journal of Legal Studies*, 12, 195–236.
Grahl, J. & Teague, P. (1994) 'Economic Citizenship in the New Europe', *Political Quarterly*, 65, 379–96.
Greenwood, S. (1992) *Britain and Economic Cooperation Since 1945* (London: Blackwell).
Guyer, P. (1993) *Kant and the Experience of Freedom: Essays on Aesthetics and Morality* (Cambridge: Cambridge University Press).
Habermas, J. (1992) 'Citizenship and National Identity: Some Reflections on the Future of Europe', *Praxis International*, 12, 1–19.
Hall, S. (1991) 'The European Convention on Human Rights and the Public Policy Exceptions to the Free Movement of Workers under the

EEC Treaty', *European Law Review,* 16, 466–88.
Harden, I. (1990) 'Sovereignty and the EuroFed', *Political Quarterly,* 61, 402–14.
Harden, I. (1994) 'The Constitution of the European Union', *Public Law,* 609–24.
Hart, H. (1961) *The Concept of Law* (Oxford: Clarendon Press).
Hartley, T. (1993) 'Constitutional and Institutional Aspects of the Maastricht Agreement', *International and Comparative Law Quarterly,* 42, 213–376.
Harvie, C. (1994) *The Rise of Regional Europe* (London: Routledge).
Heater, D. (1992) *The Idea of European Unity* (Leicester: Leicester University Press).
Heidegger, M. (1977) *The Question Concerning Technology and Other Essays* (New York: Harper).
Heller, A. & Feher, F. (1988) *The Postmodern Political Condition* (Cambridge: Polity Press).
Hilf, M. (1983) 'The Application of Rules of National Administrative Law in the Implementation of Community Law', *Yearbook of European Law,* 3, 79–98.
Hill, C. (1986) *Puritanism and Revolution* (Harmondsworth: Peregrine).
Hirst, P. (1993) *The Pluralist Theory of State: Selected Writings of G.D.H. Cole, J.N. Figgis and H.J. Laski* (London: Routledge).
Hix, S. (1994) 'The Study of the European Community: The Challenge to Comparative Politics', *West European Politics,* 17, 1–30.
Hobbes, T. (1985) *Leviathan* (Harmondsworth: Penguin).
Hoffmann, S. (1995) *The European Sisyphus: Essays on Europe 1964–1994* (Boulder, CO: Westview).
Holland, M. (1993) *European Integration: From Community to Union* (London: Pinter).
Holland, S. (1980) *UnCommon Market* (London: Macmillan).
Holland, S. (1993) *The European Imperative: Economic and Social Cohesion in the 1990s* (London: Spokesman).
Hornsby, S. (1987) 'Competition Policy in the 80s: More Policy less Competition?', *European Law Review,* 12, 79–101.
Horsman, M. & Marshall, A. (1995) *After the Nation-State: Citizens, Tribalism and New World Disorder* (London: Harper Collins).
Howe, G. (1995) 'Sovereignty, Democracy and Human Rights', *Political Quarterly,* 66, 127–37.
Howe, P. (1995) 'A Community of Europeans: The Requisite Underpinnings', *Journal of Common Market Studies,* 33, 27–45.
Hunt, A. (1990) 'The Big Fear: Law Confronts Postmodernism', *McGill Law Journal,* 35, 507–40.
Hunt, A. (1993) *Explorations in Law and Society: Towards a Constitutive Theory of Law* (London: Routledge).
Husbands, C. (1992) 'The Other Face of 1992', *Parliamentary Affairs,* 45, 267–84.
Hutchinson, A. (1988) *Dwelling on the Threshold* (Toronto: Carswell).
Hutchinson, A. (1989) 'The Three "R"s: Reading/Rorty/Radically', *Harvard Law Review,* 103, 555–85.

Ingram, A. (1993) 'The Empire Strikes Back: Liberal Solidarity in a *Europe des Patries*', in M. Karlsson (ed.), *Law, Justice and the State* (Berlin: Duncker & Humblot).

Kant, I. (1991) *The Critique of Judgement* (Oxford: Oxford University Press).

Kastendiek, H. (1990) 'Convergence or a Persistent Diversity of National Politics?', in C. Crouch & D. Marquand (eds.), *The Politics of 1992: Beyond the Single European Market* (London: Blackwell).

Kennedy, D. (1982) 'Legal Education as Training for Hierarchy', in D. Kairys (ed.), *The Politics of Law: A Progressive Critique* (New York: Pantheon).

Kenyon, J. (1966) *The Stuart Constitution* (Cambridge: Cambridge University Press).

Klare, K. (1982a) 'The Quest for Industrial Democracy and the Struggle against Racism: Perspectives from Labor Law and Civil Rights Law', *Oregon Law Review*, 61, 157–200.

Klare, K. (1982b) 'Critical Theory and Labor Relations Law', in D. Kairys (ed.), *The Politics of Law: A Progressive Critique* (New York: Pantheon).

Koopmans, T. (1991) 'The Birth of European Law at the Crossroads of Tradition', *American Journal of Comparative Law*, 39, 493–507.

Koopmans, T. (1992) 'Federalism: The Wrong Debate', *Common Market Law Review*, 29, 1047–52.

Kristeva, J. (1993) *Nations Without Nationalism* (New York: Columbia University Press).

Kulms, R. (1990) 'Competition, Trade Policy and Competition Policy in the EEC: The Example of Antidumping', *Common Market Law Review*, 27, 285–313.

Ladrech, R. (1993) 'Parliamentary Democracy and Political Discourse in EC Institutional Change', *Journal of European Integration*, 17, 53–69.

Lange, D. & Sandage, J. (1989) 'The *Woodpulp* Decision and its Implications for the Scope of EC Competition Law', *Common Market Law Review*, 26, 137–65.

Laurent, P. (1989) 'Historical Perspectives on Early European Integration', *Journal of European Integration*, 12, 89–100.

Lenaerts, K.(1991) 'Fundamental Rights to be Included in a Community Catalogue', *European Law Review*, 16, 376–89.

Lessnoff, M. (1986) *Social Contract* (London: Macmillan).

Llobera, J. (1993) 'The Role of the State and Nation in Europe', in S. Garcia (ed.), *European Identity and the Search for Legitimacy* (London: Pinter).

Locke, J. (1989) *Two Treatises of Government* (London: J.M. Dent).

Lodge, J. (1984) 'European Union and the First Elected European Parliament', *Journal of Common Market Studies*, 22, 387–92.

Lodge, J. (1986) 'The Single European Act', in J. Lodge (ed.), *European Union: The European Community in Search of a Future* (London: St Martin's Press).

Lodge, J. (1990) 'Social Europe', *Journal of European Integration*, 13, 135–50.

Lodge, J. (1993) 'Towards a Political Union?', in J. Lodge (ed.), *The European Community and the Challenge of the Future* (London: Pinter).

Lynch, F. (1993) 'Restoring France: The Road to Integration', in A. Milward et al., *The Frontier of National Sovereignty: History and Theory 1945–1992* (London: Routledge).

Lyotard, J.-F. (1984a) 'The Differend, the Referent, and the Proper Name', *Diacritics*, 14, 4–14.

Lyotard, J.-F. (1984b) *The Postmodern Condition: A Report on Knowledge* (Manchester: Manchester University Press).

Lyotard, J.-F. (1988) *The Differend* (Manchester: Manchester University Press).

Lyotard, J.-F. (1990) *Heidegger and the 'Jews'* (Minneapolis: University of Minnesota Press).

Lyotard, J.-F. (1992) 'Sensus Communis', in A. Benjamin (ed.), *Judging Lyotard* (London: Routledge).

Lyotard, J.-F. (1993a) 'Heidegger and the 'Jews': A Conference in Vienna and Freiburg', in *Political Writings* (London: University College Press).

Lyotard, J.-F. (1993b) 'The Other's Rights', in S. Shute & S. Hurley (eds.), *On Human Rights: The Oxford Amnesty Lectures 1993* (London: Basic Books).

MacCormick, N. (1981) *H.L.A. Hart* (London: Edward Arnold).

MacCormick, N. (1993) 'Beyond the Sovereign State', *Modern Law Review*, 56, 1–18.

Mackenzie Stuart, Lord (1987) 'Recent Developments in English Administrative Law – The Impact of Europe?', in F. Caportorti (ed.), *Du Droit international au droit de l'intégration: liber amoricum Pierre Pescatore* (Berlin: Steiner).

Mackenzie Stuart, Lord (1992) 'Subsidiarity – A Busted Flush?' in D. Curtin & D. O'Keeffe (eds.), *Constitutional Adjudication in European Community Law and National Law* (London: Butterworths).

MacKinnon, C. (1989) *Toward a Feminist Theory of State* (Cambridge, MA: Harvard University Press).

MacKinnon, C. (1991) 'Reflections on Sex Equality Law', *Yale Law Journal*, 100, 1281–328.

MacShane, D. (1995) 'Europe's Next Challenge to British Politics', *Political Quarterly*, 66, 23–35.

Majury, D. (1991) 'Strategizing In Equality', in M. Fineman & N. Thomadsen (eds.), *At the Boundaries of Law: Feminism and Legal Theory* (London: Routledge).

Mancini, F. (1991) 'The Making of a Constitution for Europe', in R. Keohance & S. Hoffmann (eds.), *The New European Community: Decisionmaking and Institutional Change* (Boulder, CO: Westview).

Mazey, S. (1988) 'European Community Action on Behalf of Women: The Limits of Legislation', *Journal of Common Market Studies*, 27, 63–84.

McGee, A. & Weatherill, S. (1990) 'The Evolution of the Single Market – Harmonisation or Liberalisation?', *Modern Law Review*, 53, 578–96.

McGlynn, C. (1995) 'European Works Councils: Towards Industrial Democracy?', *Industrial Law Journal*, 24, 78–84.

Meehan, E. (1990) 'Sex Equality Policies in the European Community', *Journal of European Integration*, 13, 185–96.

Milward, A. (1992) *The European Rescue of the Nation-State* (London: Routledge).
Milward, A. & Soerensen, V. (1993) 'Interdependence or Integration? A National Choice', in A. Milward et al., *The Frontier of National Sovereignty: History and Theory 1945–1992* (London: Routledge).
Monnet, J. (1978) *Memoirs* (London: Collins).
Montagnon. P. (1990) 'Conclusion', in P. Montagnon (ed.), *European Competition Policy* (London: PIIA/Pinter).
Moravcsik, A. (1994) 'Preferences and Power in the European Community: A Liberal Intergovernmentalist Approach', in S. Bulmer & R. Scott (eds.), *Economic and Political Integration: Internal Dynamics and Global Context* (London: Blackwell).
More, G. (1993) '"Equal Treatment" of the Sexes in European Community Law: What Does "Equal" Mean?', *Feminist Legal Studies*, 1, 45–74.
Moxon-Browne, E. (1993) 'Social Europe', in J. Lodge (ed.), *The European Community and the Challenge of the Future* (London: Pinter).
Mueller-Graff, P. (1994) 'The Legal Basis of the Third Pillar and its Position in the Framework of the Union Treaty', *Common Market Law Review*, 31, 493–510.
Munro, C. (1987) *Studies in Constitutional Law* (London: Butterworths).
Nascimbene, R. (1992) 'The Albanians in Italy: The Right of Asylum under Attack?', *International Journal of Refugee Law*, 3, 714–20.
Nicoll, W. (1984) 'The Luxembourg Compromise', *Journal of Common Market Studies*, 23, 35–43.
Nicoll, W. (1994) 'Representing the States', in A. Duff, J. Pinder & R. Pryce (eds.), *Maastricht and Beyond: Building the European Union* (London: Routledge).
Nicholls, D. (1994) *The Pluralist State* (London: Macmillan).
O'Keeffe, D. (1991) 'The Schengen Convention: A Suitable Model for European Integration?', *Yearbook of European Law*, 11, 185–219.
O'Keeffe, D. (1992) 'The Free Movement of Persons and the Single Market', *European Law Review*, 17, 3–19.
O'Keeffe, D. (1994) 'Union Citizenship', in D. O'Keeffe & P. Twomey (eds.), *Legal Issues of the Maastricht* (London: Chancery Press).
O'Keeffe, D. (1995) 'The Emergence of a European Immigration Policy', *European Law Review*, 20, 20–36.
O'Leary, S. (1995) 'The Relationship between Community Citizenship and the Protection of Fundamental Rights in Community Law', *Common Market Law Review*, 32, 519–54.
Oliver, D. (1994) 'What is Happening to Relationships Between the Individual and the State', in J. Jowell & D. Oliver (eds.), *The Changing Constitution* (Oxford: Oxford University Press).
Papandreou, V. (1990) 'Free Movement of Qualified Labour: A Commissioner's Perspective', *Journal of European Integration*, 13. 197–202.
Paul, R. (1992) 'Black and Third World Peoples' Citizenship and 1992', *Critical Social Policy*, 11, 52–65.
Pescatore, P. (1987) 'Some Critical Remarks on the Single European Act', *Common Market Law Review*, 24, 9–18.
Peterson, J. (1994) 'Subsidiarity: A Definition to Suit Any Vision?' *Parliamentary Affairs*, 47, 116–32.

Phelan, D. (1992) 'Right to Life of the Unborn v Promotion of Trade in Services: The European Court of Justice and the Normative Shaping of the European Union', *Modern Law Review*, 55, 670–89.

Picht, R. (1993) 'Disturbed Identities: Social and Cultural Mutations in Contemporary Europe', in S. Garcia (ed.), *European Identity and the Search for Legitimacy* (London: Pinter).

Pinder, J. (1991) 'The European Community, the Rule of Law and Representative Government: The Significance of the Intergovernmental Conferences', *Government and Opposition*, 26, 199–214.

Pinder, J. (1993) 'The Single Market: A Step Towards Union', in J. Lodge (ed.), *The European Community and the Challenge of the Future* (London: Pinter).

Pinder, J. (1994) 'Building the Union: Policy, Reform, Constitution', in A. Duff, J. Pinder & R. Pryce (eds.), *Maastricht and Beyond: Building the European Union* (London: Routledge).

Postema, G. (1986) *Bentham and the Common Law Tradition* (Oxford: Clarendon Press).

Ransome, P. (1991) *Towards the United States of Europe* (London: Lothian Foundation).

Rasmussen, H. (1986) *On Law and Policy in the European Court of Justice: A Comparative Study in Judicial Policymaking* (Dordrecht: Martinus Nijhoff).

Rawlings, R. (1993) 'The Eurolaw Game: Some Deductions from a Saga', *Journal of Law and Society*, 20, 309–40.

Rawls, J. (1973) *A Theory of Justice* (Oxford: Oxford University Press).

Rawls, J. (1993a) *Political Liberalism* (New York: Columbia University Press).

Rawls, J. (1993b) 'The Law of Peoples', in S. Shute & S. Hurley (eds.), *On Human Rights: The Oxford Amnesty Lectures 1993* (London: Basic Books).

Raworth, P. (1994) 'A Timid Step Forwards: Maastricht and the Democratisation of Europe' *European Law Review*, 19, 16–33.

Reif, K. (1993) 'Cultural Divergence and Cultural Diversity as Factors in European Identity', in A. Garcia (ed.), *European Identity and the Search for Legitimacy* (London: Pinter).

Rhode, D. (1989) *Justice and Gender* (Cambridge, Mass.: Harvard University Press).

Rhode, D. (1990) 'Feminist Critical Studies', *Stanford Law Review*, 42, 617–38.

Romero, F. (1993) 'Migration as an Issue in European Interdepence and Integration: The Case of Italy', in A. Milward et al., *The Frontier of National Sovereignty: History and Theory 1945–1992* (London: Routledge).

Rorty, R. (1980) *Philosophy and the Mirror of Nature* (Princeton, NJ: Princeton University Press).

Rorty, R. (1989) *Contingency, Irony, and Solidarity* (Cambridge: Cambridge University Press).

Rorty, R. (1991) *Essays on Heidegger and Others* (Cambridge: Cambridge University Press).

Rorty, R. (1993) 'Human Rights, Rationality, and Sentimentality', in S. Shute & S. Hurley (eds.), *On Human Rights: The Oxford Amnesty Lectures 1993* (London: Basic Books).

Ruggie, J. (1993) 'Territoriality and Beyond: Problematizing Modernity in International Relations', *International Organization*, 47, 165–80.

Scheiwe, K. (1994) 'EC Law's Unequal Treatment of the Family: The Case Law of the European Court of Justice on Rules Prohibiting Discrimination on Grounds of Sex and Nationality', *Social and Legal Studies*, 3, 243–65.

Schermers, H. (1990) 'The Scales in the Balance: National Constitutional Court v Court of Justice', *Common Market Law Review*, 27, 97–105.

Schwarze, J. (1986) 'The Administrative Law of the Community and the Protection of Human Rights', *Common Market Law Review*, 23, 410–17.

Schwarze, J. (1991) 'Tendencies Towards a Common Administrative Law in Europe', *European Law Review*, 16, 3–19.

Schwarze, J. (1992) *European Administrative Law* (London: Sweet & Maxwell).

Sciortino, G. (1991) 'Immigration into Europe and Public Policy: Do Stops Really Work?', *New Community*, 18, 89–99.

Scott, J. (1992) 'European Law', in I. Grigg-Spall & P. Ireland (eds.), *The Critical Lawyer's Handbook* (London: Pluto Press).

Scott, J. (1995) *Development Dilemmas in the European Community: Rethinking Regional Development Policy* (Milton Keynes: Open University Press).

Shaw, J. (1994) 'Twin-Track Social Europe – the Inside Track', in D. O'Keeffe & P. Twomey (eds.), *Legal Issues of the Maastricht Treaty* (London: Chancery Press).

Slater, M. (1982) 'Political Elites, Popular Indifference and Community Building', *Journal of Common Market Studies*, 21, 69–93.

Slynn, G. (1987) 'But in England there is no . . .', in W. Furst (ed.), *Festschrift für Wolfgang Zeidler* (Berlin: de Gruyter).

Smith, A. (1992) 'National Identity and the Idea of European Unity', *International Affairs*, 68, 55–76.

Smith, T. (1994) 'Post-Modern Politics and the Case for Constitutional Renewal', *Political Quarterly*, 65, 128–37.

Snyder, F. (1990) *New Directions in European Law* (London: Weidenfeld & Nicolson).

Soerensen, V. (1993) 'Between Interdependence and Integration: Denmark's Shifting Strategies', in A. Milward et al., *The Frontier of National Sovereignty: History and Theory 1945–1992* (London: Routledge).

Sohrab, J. (1994) 'Women and Social Security: the Limits of EEC Equality Law', *Journal of Social Welfare and Family Law*, 5–17.

Speck, W. (1988) *Reluctant Revolutionaries* (Oxford: Oxford University Press).

Spencer, M. (1995) *States of Injustice* (London: Pluto Press).

Spicker, P. (1991) 'The Principles of Subsidiarity and the Social Policy of the European Community', *Journal of European Social Policy*, 1, 3–14.

Stein, E. (1983) 'The European Community in 1983: A Less Perfect Union?', *Common Market Law Review*, 20, 641–56.

Steiner, J. (1993) 'From Direct Effects to *Francovich*: Shifting Means of Enforcement of Community Law', *European Law Review*, 18, 3–22.

Story, J. (1990) 'Europe's Future: Western Europe or Common Home?', in C. Crouch & D. Marquand (eds.), *The Politics of 1992: Beyond the Single European Market* (London: Blackwell).

Szyszczak, E. (1994) 'Social Policy: A Happy Ending or a Reworking of the Fairy Tale?', in D. O'Keeffe & P. Twomey (eds.), *Legal Issues of the Maastricht Treaty* (London: Chancery Press).

Tatham, A. (1991) 'Effect of European Community Directives: The Development of the *Cohn-Bendit* Jurisprudence', *International and Comparative Law Quarterly*, 40, 907–19.

Teague, P. (1989) *The European Community: The Social Dimension* (Cranfield: Cranfield Institute).

Teague, P. (1993) 'Coordination or Decentralization? EC Social Policy and European Industrial Relations', in J. Lodge (ed.), *The European Community and the Challenge of the Future* (London: Pinter).

Teasdale, A. (1993) 'Subsidiarity in Post-Maastricht Europe', *Political Quarterly*, 64, 187–97.

Therborn, G. (1995) *European Modernity and Beyond* (London: Sage).

Thompson, J. (1992) *Justice and World Order* (London: Routledge).

Toth, A. (1992) 'The Principle of Subsidiarity in the Maastricht Treaty', *Common Market Law Review*, 29, 1079–105.

Toth, A. (1994) 'Is Subsidiarity Justiciable?', *European Law Review*, 19, 268–85.

Tsoukalis, L. (1991) *The New European Economy: The Politics and Economics of European Integration* (Oxford: Oxford University Press).

Twomey, P. (1994) 'The European Union: Three Pillars without a Human Rights Foundation', in D. O'Keeffe & P. Twomey (eds.), *Legal Issues of the Maastricht Treaty* (London: Chancery Press).

Unger, R. (1987) *Politics, A Work in Constructive Social Theory* (Cambridge: Cambridge University Press).

Urwin, D. (1995) *The Community of Europe* (London: Longman).

Volcansek, M. (1992) 'The European Court of Justice: Supranational Policy-Making', *West European Politics*, 15, 109–21.

Wade, W. (1991) 'What has Happened to the Sovereignty of Parliament?', *Law Quarterly Review*, 107, 1–4.

Wallace, H. (1984) 'European Governance in Turbulent Times', in S. Bulmer & S. Scott (eds.), *Economic and Political Integration in Europe: Internal Dynamics and Global Context* (London: Blackwell).

Wallace, H. (1993) 'Deepening and Widening: Problems of Legitimacy for the EC', in S. Garcia (ed.), *European Identity and the Search for Legitimacy* (London: Pinter).

Wallace, H. (1995) 'Britain out on a Limb?', *Political Quarterly*, 66, 46–58.

Warbrick, C. (1994) 'Rights, the European Convention on Human Rights and English Law', *European Law Review*, 19, 34–46.

Ward, I. (1993) 'Making Sense of Integration: A Philosophy of Law for the European Community', *Journal of European Integration*, 17, 101–36.

Ward, I. (1994a) 'The Best of All Possible Worlds?: Maastricht and the United Kingdom', *Indiana International and Comparative Law Review*, 5, 75–99.

Ward, I. (1994b) 'The Anomalous, the Wrong and the Unhappy: UK Administrative Law in a European Perspective', *Northern Ireland Legal Quarterly*, 45, 46–52.

Ward, I. (1994c) 'The Story of M: A Cautionary Tale from the United Kingdom', *International Journal of Refugee Law*, 6, 194–206.

Ward, I. (1994d) 'The Sorceror and His Apprentices: Kant and the Critical Legal Project', *Archiv für Rechts- und Sozialphilosophie*, 80, 508–33.

Ward, I. (1995) 'Another Look at the New Rawls', *Anglo-American Law Review*, 24, 104–22.

Watson, P. (1995) 'Equality of Treatment: A Variable Concept?', *Industrial Law Journal*, 24, 33–48.

Weatherill, S. & Beaumont, P. (1993) *EC Law* (Harmondsworth, Penguin).

Weigall, D. & Stirk, P. (eds.) (1992) *The Origins and Development of the European Community* (Leicester: Leicester University Press).

Weiler, J. (1986) 'Eurocracy and Distrust: Some Questions Concerning the Role of the European Court of Justice in the Protection of Fundamental Rights within the Legal Order of the European Communities', *Washington Law Review*, 61, 1103–42.

Weiler, J. (1991a) 'The Transformation of Europe', *Yale Law Journal*, 100, 2403–83.

Weiler, J. (1991b) 'Problems of Legitimacy in post-1992 Europe', *Aussenwirtschaft*, 46, 411–37.

Weiler, J. (1992) 'Thou Shalt Not Oppress a Stranger: On the Judicial Protection of the Human Rights of non-EC Nationals – A Critique', *European Journal of International Law*, 3, 65–90.

Weiler, J. & Lockhart, N. (1995) '"Taking Rights Seriously" Seriously: The European Court and its Fundamental Rights Jurisprudence', *Common Market Law Review*, 32, 51–94 & 579–627.

Williams, A. (1991) *The European Community* (London: Blackwell).

Williams, J. (1991) 'Dissolving the Sameness/Difference Debate: A Post-Modern Path beyond Essentialism in Feminist and Critical Race Theory', *Duke Law Journal*, 296–323.

Williams, P. (1987) 'Alchemical Notes: Reconstructing Ideals from Deconstructed Rights', *Harvard Civil Rights-Civil Liberties Review*, 22, 401–33.

Williams, S. (1991) 'Sovereignty and Accountability in the European Community', R. Keohane & S. Hoffmann (eds.), *The New European Community: Decisionmaking and Institutional Change* (Boulder, CO: Westview).

Wise, M. & Gibb, R. (1993) *Single Market to Social Europe* (London: Longman).

Wistrich, E. (1994) *The United States of Europe* (London: Routledge).

Wyatt, D. & Dashwood, A. (1993) *European Community Law* (London: Sweet & Maxwell).

Young, J. (1993) *Britain and European Unity: 1945–1992* (London: Macmillan).

Index